PUFFIN B...

Tell No One Who You Are

Régine Miller was born in Brussels in 1932 of Polish-Jewish immigrants. She was hidden for nearly three years during the Nazi occupation, and after the war went to live with an uncle in England. At the age of eighteen she married a survivor of the Buchenwald concentration camp with whom she had two children. In 1958 the family emigrated to Canada. Perfectly bilingual in English and French, Régine worked as an editorial assistant and translator in Montreal where she still lives with her daughter, Sonia. Her son, Philip, is a lawyer living in Ontario, Canada.

Walter Buchignani was a twenty-eight-year-old reporter for the *Montreal Gazette* when he met Régine Miller. At the time he was covering a 1991 gathering in New York of Jewish children who had been hidden from the Nazis during the Second World War. Because he was neither Jewish, nor even born when the Holocaust took place, he set out to understand the survivors both factually and emotionally and to write about them in the kind of detail that helps readers to understand. This is his first book.

113

Walter Buchignani

Tell No One Who You Are

PUFFIN BOOKS

PUFFIN BOOKS

Published by the Penguin Group
Penguin Books Ltd, 27 Wrights Lane, London W8 5TZ, England
Penguin Books USA Inc., 375 Hudson Street, New York, New York 10014, USA
Penguin Books Australia Ltd, Ringwood, Victoria, Australia
Penguin Books Canada Ltd, 10 Alcorn Avenue, Toronto, Ontario, Canada M4V 3B2
Penguin Books (NZ) Ltd, 182–190 Wairau Road, Auckland 10, New Zealand

Penguin Books Ltd, Registered Offices: Harmondsworth, Middlesex, England

First published in Canada by Tundra Books 1994
Published in Puffin Books 1997
1 3 5 7 9 10 8 6 4 2

This edition published by arrangement with Tundra Books, Toronto, Canada

The moral right of the author has been asserted

Made and printed in England by Clays Ltd, St Ives plc

Foreword

THE WAR IN EUROPE had been going on for months, but for Régine Miller it started just after breakfast on a Friday in the spring of 1940. She was eight years old.

Régine already knew a little about war. Every evening since Germany invaded Poland the previous September, she sat with her parents near the radio and listened to the news. Her parents had left Poland and come to Belgium when her older brother Léon was a baby. They lived in a district of Brussels among other Jewish immigrants, and everyone seemed to have relatives back in Poland. Whenever neighbors met on the street, they asked if anyone had news from those left behind. Régine's grandparents on her mother's side lived near Warsaw. She had learned the Hebrew alphabet from her father so she could write a few words in Yiddish to them, but since the war began she had not received a letter back.

The war caused other problems. Her mother spoke of how little food there was in the market when they went shopping. "The war is doing it," she said. Fathers of school friends were out of work "because of the war." Her own father brought home less work than before.

The war was blamed on Adolf Hitler and the Germans. She saw his picture on the front page of newspapers. She heard his name spoken with anger and fear on the streets and among the teachers at school. Only her father seemed not to be afraid. He was sure it would all end soon. "Hitler wants to take over the world, but he'll be stopped. England and France will stop him."

In spite of all the talk, war to Régine was something bad that went on in other places. This war was in Poland. There had been a previous war in Spain.* She knew about the war there when she was five years old. She had watched her father pack boxes of food and clothes donated by Jewish families "to help the people of Spain." This was part of his volunteer work with a group called Solidarité.

Régine did not understand much of what went on at the Solidarité gatherings. They took place in the homes of the members and there was a lot of talking. Régine's mother did not like Régine going there. "She's too young to go to political meetings," she complained. But her father said it was never too early to learn about politics and how to make the world a better place.

Sitting beside her father, pleased to be with him, Régine could feel how serious this new, bigger war was to the members of Solidarité as they talked about what was being done to "stop Hitler and the Germans." While reports were given on the fighting, on people killed and people rescued, she liked to watch one of the women in particular. Her name was Fela; she was pretty and sure of herself and had a nice way of speaking. Régine wanted to be like that when she grew up.

This new war was killing people, even children. But like that other war in Spain, it went on far away. Until that Friday morning. When war started for Régine, it did not start with the sound of guns, bombs or planes. It started with the noise of her brother's feet running up the stairs.

* The Spanish Civil War 1936-1939

Chapter One

IT WAS NOT YET 7 a.m. but Régine's day had already begun. She had helped her mother clear the breakfast dishes and was getting ready for school. She set down her schoolbag on the kitchen table and filled it with exercise books. She collected her pencils, dropped them into her wooden pencil box and slid the lid closed, then placed the box in her schoolbag and fastened the leather straps.

"Haven't you left yet?" her father called from the other room. She could see him through the open door, bent over the black sewing machine with which he earned his living.

"Almost ready, Papa." She went to where he was working, leaned over and kissed him on both cheeks.

The sewing machine and a large table took up most of the workroom in the apartment at 73 rue Van Lint. Handbags were piled on the table ready to be taken to the company that provided the leather and paid her father for each bag he cut and sewed. In the neighborhood, Maurice Miller was known as a *maroquinier*, a leather worker.

Régine stood, watching him sew a small piece of leather. "You still here?" he asked, looking up at her.

"I'm leaving. I'm leaving."

She returned to the kitchen where her mother was wiping the table. "Why is Papa always worrying? I'm never late." She kissed her mother, grabbed her schoolbag and was about to go out the door.

The *école primaire* — elementary school — Régine attended was just a few minutes' walk along rue Van Lint. Not like her brother's school. Léon Miller was fourteen and had to take the tram to get to his *école moyenne* — secondary school. He left the apartment early and traveled with his best friend, a boy who was also called Léon. His family, the Saktregers, lived on rue Van Lint only six doors away from the Millers. They also had a son Régine's age named Maurice who sometimes came to the Millers' with his brother.

On school days, by the time Régine got out of bed, her brother had already left and she would not see him until suppertime. That's why on this particular morning she was surprised to hear his footsteps running up the hallway stairs. The apartment door flew open and she jumped out of the way to avoid being hit as he rushed in. The noise brought her mother from the kitchen and her father from his workroom.

"Léon, what's wrong?" her father asked.

"No school today," her brother said, out of breath.

"Why? What happened?"

"School is canceled," he said. "All the schools are closed. And all the shops. Nothing is open."

Régine's mother let out a cry and covered her mouth to stifle it. Régine looked at her father, expecting him to explain. But he stood silent with his head bowed as he had done the night before while listening to the news on the radio. His whole body seemed to tighten and he closed his eyes as if to clear his head. Régine kept looking at him. Before that day, if you had asked her about the war, she would have tossed her red hair and said it would soon be over. Her father had told her so. Now hearing her mother cry out and seeing the look on her father's face, for the first time she felt frightened.

It was May 10, 1940, the date history would record as the day the Germans invaded Belgium.

4

Chapter Two

THAT FRIDAY not only marked the beginning of war for Régine, it also divided the "before" and "after" of her life. It was only later when she thought back to "before the war" that she realized her family had been poor. She had never felt poor.

Sana Moszek Miller and his wife, Zlata Miller, had left Poland and come to Belgium because they dreamed of a better life, if not for themselves, at least for their children. They believed the way to that better life was through education. They wanted their children to be good Belgians and even though Yiddish was the language of their mother, Mr. Miller always spoke French to the children. He even took the French version of his name, Maurice.

Léon and Régine were never allowed to stay home from school unless they were very ill. Sometimes they had to help their father late into the night because there was more work than he could finish, but they had to do their lessons first and were not allowed to skip school the next day.

Her father worked long days, starting before Régine left for school in the morning and continuing long after she returned in the afternoon. When the others helped, they stood at the long cutting table in the workroom. Léon and Mrs. Miller cut out the leather patterns with huge scissors while Régine scooped glue out of a jar and applied it to the pieces. Her father did all the sewing, bent over his machine and working the treadle, his face inches away from the needle.

There were only two other rooms in their second-floor flat. The windows looked onto the cobblestone street. In summer it was stuffy and, when the windows were open, noisy from the trams passing. Downstairs was a café and the sounds of comings and goings also drifted upstairs.

Régine slept in the same room as her parents, in the crib she had used as a baby. She could not stretch her legs in it; she slept on her side, her knees bent to her chest. She had done this for so long, she found nothing strange or uncomfortable about it. Next to her parents' bed was another small sewing machine where her mother did the family mending.

Léon did not have a proper bed, either. He slept on a sofa in the main room that was both a living room and a kitchen with two stoves. A gas stove was used for cooking, and in the winter Léon had the job of feeding the heating stove. He carried the heavy shovelfuls of coal from where it was stored out in the hall in a closet under the stairs that led to the third floor.

He did not seem to need much sleep. When he finished his homework, if he didn't have to help in the workroom, he liked to go out with the other Léon and their friends. Régine would listen from her crib for him to come in, see the light go on under the door to the main room and know that he was reading the library books he brought home.

The most imposing piece of furniture in the main room was a wooden radio with large, round dials and four short legs. Régine's mother turned on the radio first thing in the morning and shut it off before going to bed at night. The music seemed to help her now that she was ill and went out only to shop for food.

Régine had loved to go shopping with her mother before she got sick. At the fishmonger's, Mrs. Miller prodded the fish and studied the eyes to decide if it was fresh enough. She was equally fussy with chickens, which she brought home from the market freshly killed according to Jewish law. She plucked the feathers and held the chicken over a flame to burn off ends that clung to the skin. Then came the ritual of soaking it in salted water to get rid of all traces of blood. The neck was stuffed before roasting in the oven, and Régine liked eating that part best.

Her mother still shopped carefully, but lately she seemed in a hurry to get home and lie down to rest before starting supper. Régine liked to help. She learned to crush almonds with a mortar and pestle for apple cake and make dough for noodles. The dough had to be stretched over a white table-cloth until it was paper thin. It was left to dry and later cut into narrow strips, ready to be cooked and eaten in chicken soup.

While they worked together her mother asked how school had gone that day. She wanted all the details, not just what she had learned, what her marks were, but what songs they had sung and whether they had played hopscotch at recess. She told Régine she was lucky to have such a good teacher as Mademoiselle Descotte. But Régine knew that.

Before getting sick her mother had been very busy and popular with the other Jewish mothers in the neighborhood. They asked her how to cook certain dishes, what to give a sick child and sometimes even asked her to help settle an argument. She seemed to have time for everyone then. But now she was always tired.

On that Friday morning when Léon ran in, her mother started to tremble after crying out. She looked about to faint and Mr. Miller and Léon helped her onto a chair so she could sit down.

When she was able to speak, she put out her hand to her

husband. "Maurice," she said, "you should have gone to England when I begged you."

Régine knew what came next. Her father had been sure the war would end before it got to Belgium, but her mother had always been afraid. When the Germans invaded Poland, her mother had pleaded with him to go to England where her brother Shlomo lived. "Belgium is a small country," she had argued. "The Germans came here in the last war. If they do it again, they will take you away."

"I'm not leaving you," her father said each time the argument started.

"But it's you they'll take. They want men to work for them. They won't touch me or the children."

That morning, as Régine and Léon stood watching, her mother tried again. She was almost in tears as she begged: "It's not too late. Why don't you go, now? I hear people have been escaping through France in the last few days. Please."

Her father tried to sound his old calm self: "I'm staying with you and I'm staying to fight. If everybody leaves who will fight them?"

"Fight them?" her mother cried. "What can you do? You and your Solidarité friends. You think you help with those tracts urging people to resist the Germans? You think you can stop them by blowing up a few bridges and rail lines? And if they catch you, they'll..." She broke into sobs and could not finish.

Her father put his arm around her mother and his voice was gentle. "It's no use, Zlata. I'm staying with you, no matter what."

Chapter Three

A FEW DAYS after the invasion, Régine saw German soldiers for the first time. She watched, standing at the apartment window with her father and mother, as they marched past, parading through the city, showing off their power.

"What will they do to us?" Régine asked.

Her father pursed his lips together and did not answer.

Everyone seemed to talk less. The schools reopened, but the teachers spoke to each other in whispers, as if they did not want to be overheard.

As soon as the shops opened, there was a rush on them. Housewives bought as much as they could carry, as if expecting that the following day there would be no food left to buy. Often there was very little, only rutabagas. Régine's mother brought home *pain d'épice*, a kind of honey cake with ginger that would not easily go stale. And rutabagas. Coffee, loved by everyone in Belgium, including her parents, was no longer to be had. Instead the family drank a substitute made from chicory and malt. The only plentiful food was rutabagas, and Régine hated the vegetable.

She had always been a finicky eater, but as the war went on she stopped being finicky. For the first time in her life, she felt hunger. Léon suffered even more. He was a teenager and always hungry. The small rations became smaller. Before the war, the baker nearby sold all kinds of delicious bread. Now the only bread was gray and sticky. The once plentiful red potatoes that used to arrive by train from Poland were difficult to come by, and the few that turned up in the shops were often rotten. Meat rations were tiny and had to last for an entire week. Then, in October, the Germans outlawed the killing of animals according to religious laws. "It's bad enough we have so little meat," Mrs. Miller said. "Now we can't have it kosher."

But Régine's family would soon have worse things to worry about.

Chapter Four

THE BRITISH AIR FORCE started to bomb areas in Europe held by the Germans.

One afternoon Régine helped her father place wide strips of tape across the windows in the apartment. She held the roll as he pulled and stretched the tape across the glass in the shape of an X. Her mother and Léon did the same at the other window. Soon both windows were marked with an X so that if bombs fell nearby, the glass would not shatter.

At night they hung a large, dark blanket in each window. It covered the glass so that no light shone outside. The Germans imposed this regulation so enemy bombers attacking at night would see nothing but darkness below and simply fly over.

The first time the bombers came, the sound of the air-raid sirens was terrifying, a loud, wailing noise in the distance. Her father turned out all the lights in the apartment and then crept to one of the windows. Pulling up a corner of the blanket, he peered through the small opening. Régine joined him while her mother and brother stood at the other window.

"Look!" said her father, pointing to the full moon. "There's some light after all!"

In the eerie glow the buildings seemed like shadows on the deserted street. Off in the distance, the air-raid sirens continued their slow wailing.

Then Régine heard another sound, a slow, rumbling noise

coming from far off. She looked up at her father and saw from his expression that he had heard it too. He peeled back more of the blanket and bent down to have a better view of the sky. Now there was no mistaking the rumbling: it was getting closer, growing louder and louder, until it drowned out the sound of the sirens. Régine covered her ears. Her father nudged her to bend down and look where he was pointing.

"There. Up in the sky. See?"

The planes approached, silhouetted against the sky. They flew in long, flowing lines, one after the other, and in the moonlight each plane looked like a giant roaring monster. Her father quickly put the corner of the blanket back into place and stepped away from the window. He pulled Régine with him, pushing her down to the floor. Her mother and brother were crouching together, away from their window, just as her father had taught them to do.

The noise was deafening. Régine held her breath and closed her eyes. She had never heard such a loud, terrifying roar. *The bombers must be directly over the building*. Her father's arms tightened around her and she clenched her fists as she waited for the sound of exploding bombs.

Time seemed to slow down. Seconds seemed like minutes as she waited. Then the roar of the last plane trailed off in the distance and the air-raid sirens sounded again. The planes were gone and the danger was over.

Régine opened her eyes but couldn't move. She was too scared.

"It's all right," her father said. He pulled her to her feet. Her brother and mother stood up. Régine let out her breath and hugged her father.

Now everyone could try to get to sleep.

The next morning, Régine helped take down the blankets from the windows. What a relief to see the sun shining and people walking in the street below. But when darkness came again, she helped put the blankets back up. This became a routine during the first weeks after the Germans arrived, except sometimes the bombers came and sometimes they didn't.

Her father tried to make her feel better about the planes. "The bombers are enemy planes only to the Germans. They will help end the war," he said. Régine had mixed feelings about the bombers. The planes were a danger, a necessary evil. They aroused both fear and hope, like the skull-and-cross-bones labels on the medicines her mother took. She was sorry her mother had to take such dangerous medicines but hoped they would make her better.

Chapter Five

THE PERSECUTION of the Jews in Belgium began a few months after the Nazis arrived. Five days after the ritual slaughter of animals was forbidden announcements ordered Jews, and anyone of Jewish origin, to register with the Nazi authorities. Their identity cards were marked in bold letters in German, Flemish and French: *Jude, Jood, Juif*.

Jews were now prohibited from working in government offices. Jews were prohibited from working as lawyers. From now on, no Jew could be employed as a journalist. Restrictions were imposed on the amount of money Jews could withdraw from their bank accounts.

The Nazis imposed the restrictions against the Jews slowly so as not to arouse the rest of the Belgian population. They waited six months before announcing their next set of restrictions. On May 31, 1941, Jewish people were told they could live only in the four largest cities in Belgium: Brussels, Antwerp, Liège and Charleroi. They could not leave their homes between 8 p.m. and 7 a.m. They were banned from riding on all but the last car on the trams and were banned altogether from the trains. On the streets, signs were posted outside Jewish-owned shops, identifying them as Jewish, again in three languages. Public buildings, from swimming pools to libraries, had notices saying: "NO ENTRY TO JEWS, NEGROES AND DOGS."

Even listening to the radio was now a crime. Jews were

no longer allowed to own radios or transmitters. The family's beloved old radio, as well as the big sewing machine, was carried out of the apartment by Régine's father and brother and taken to the home of a non-Jewish neighbor for safekeeping.

But Régine's father was still able to listen to the broadcasts from London. Every night, he climbed the stairs to the apartment above. Their neighbors, Monsieur and Madame Demers, who were not Jewish, invited him to listen to their small radio through headphones. In June, they heard of the German invasion of Russia. Régine's father returned jubilant. "That will be the end of them," he said. "Russia defeated Napoleon and it will defeat Hitler as well."

And in December when the Japanese attacked the Americans at Pearl Harbor and the U.S. entered the war, he was even more confident. "It won't last long now," he said.

But it did.

In January of 1942, it was announced that Jews were not allowed to leave the country. "You should have gone to England when you could," Mrs. Miller told her husband wearily. "Now it's too late."

One day at school, a month after her tenth birthday on March 16, 1942, Régine passed a group of teachers standing in the hallway near her classroom and she heard part of the conversation. Mademoiselle Descotte was among them. "What a disgrace," she heard her teacher tell the others. "We'll be losing some of our best students."

Régine did not know what her favorite teacher meant by this and nothing further was said about it in class. The day went on as usual at *l'école primaire*. Mademoiselle Descotte read aloud a composition that Régine had written for homework a few days before, and she flushed with embarrassment as the other students turned to look at her. Later the class sat

15

in a circle and sang songs. The voice of Mademoiselle Descotte, usually the loudest, seemed quieter. Something was wrong.

At home that night, Régine was told by her parents about the latest restriction imposed by the Germans against the Jews in Belgium. The regulation had been made four months earlier. "I guess we're lucky the Germans took this long to implement it," her father said bitterly.

Régine understood now what the teachers had been discussing in the hallway. Jewish children were prohibited from attending public schools. Régine would have to stay home, and so would Léon. "Don't worry," her father said. "It's for a little while. Soon things will be back to normal again. I promise."

That night, as the bombers flew overhead, Régine cried in her crib.

Chapter Six

A MONTH LATER, her father left the apartment shortly after the curfew lifted at 7 o'clock in the morning and returned a few hours later holding a bunch of yellow badges. He took them into his workroom without saying a word.

Régine knew all about the yellow badges. They were made of cloth in the shape of the Star of David. All Jewish people were required to wear them by order of the German authorities. The yellow star meant that the wearer was Jewish, just as the signs outside shops signified that the owners were Jewish. The radio announcer explained that the badges should be sewn on sweaters, jackets or other outer clothing where they would be clearly visible.

The badges looked awfully big when she saw them in her father's hand, and garish in their bright yellow color. No one would fail to notice them. Suddenly she felt afraid. What would it be like to be singled out this way?

The door to the workroom was open. Régine saw her father drop the badges on the table as he sat down. Then he reached into a mound of scrap material and pulled out a sheet of red felt and laid it flat in front of him. He grabbed a pencil, his scissors and the jar of glue. He picked up one of the badges, held it firmly against the red felt and traced the shape of the star. Putting the yellow badge aside, he picked up the scissors and began to cut out the red star.

Régine came up behind him. "What are you doing, Papa?"

"I'll show you."

"Can I help?"

"Here's the glue. When I finish cutting out this red star, you stick it to the back of the yellow star. Then Mama will sew it to your dress. We'll do the same with all of them, every single star."

Régine just stared at the red and yellow stars. "Why?" she asked.

Mr. Miller put down the scissors. "If you are forced to do something that you think is wrong," he said, "then you must protest. Understand?"

Régine nodded, even though she did not understand.

"The red means you don't agree with having to wear the yellow star. It says you think it's wrong. Red is the color of protest, the color of revolution."

"But no one will see it," Régine said. "The red is on the back."

"*You* know it's there," her father said. "That's what matters. It'll be your little secret."

"You mean, I can't tell anyone?"

"Not for now."

"When can I tell?"

"After the war," he said. "Then we can turn them over to show the red side. And everyone will be proud of you. Because you wore the badge in protest."

"When will the war be over?"

"Soon," her father said. "I promise."

He picked up the scissors and resumed his work of cutting the red felt in the shapes of stars. "Today Mama will sew the badges," he said. "And tomorrow — guess what we'll do."

Régine smiled and shook her head.

"Tomorrow you'll put on your nice dress and I'll take you to the photographer. He'll take a picture of you in your dress with the yellow star. Then, when all this is over, we'll go back and take one with the red star. And you will keep them as a memory of the war. And I will buy you a pair of gold earrings to celebrate."

Régine had never been to a photo studio before. She ran into the kitchen and told her mother the news. But as soon as she mentioned the red star, she knew she had made a mistake. She did not want to cause her more pain than she was already suffering. Her mother was getting sicker all the time. She had been in and out of the hospital. At home, she sometimes spent the whole day in bed. Doctor Zilbershatz, the family doctor, an elderly man with a beard, came to the apartment with more medicine jars and gave her injections. He brought his wife sometimes and never took money for his visits.

Régine watched her mother walk slowly, with difficulty, into the workroom.

"What are you teaching our daughter?" Mrs. Miller said in a high, pained voice. "What is all this talk about protests and revolution? She's too young to be involved in politics."

"One is never too young to learn about social justice," Régine heard her father say.

The next morning, she put on her best dress and walked with her father to Pierre Dietens' photo studio at 128 rue Wayez. The dress was pink and decorated with small flowers. Her mother had bought the fabric long ago, and there had been enough material to make a dress for both herself and Régine. Together they had gone to the dressmaker, Madame David, who had taken their measurements and later came to the apartment for a fitting. Régine liked to wear her dress when her mother wore hers. Whenever they walked the cobblestone streets wearing the matching dresses, Régine felt she and her mother were like sisters.

But her mother had not worn her flowered dress in a long

time. She had lost so much weight it did not fit anymore. Régine's dress still fit perfectly when she went to the photo studio, only now it bore the yellow Star of David with the red underside.

Monsieur Dietens, the photographer, brought out a stool for Régine to sit on. He told her to sit up straight and put her hands in her lap and look straight into the lens. He walked behind his camera, which was set up on a tripod, and his head disappeared under a black sheet. Without moving her head, Régine shifted her eyes to look at her father, who was standing to the side. She saw that he was smiling, and he winked at her.

"This way," Monsieur Dietens said. Régine looked into the lens of the big camera, whose front expanded and retracted like an accordion. She straightened her shoulders and was conscious of the yellow star on the left side of her chest. She smiled at the thought of the red star underneath. That's when Monsieur Dietens pressed the shutter with a terrific flash of light.

When the black and white print was ready, her father put it in a frame and hung it on the wall along with the other family photographs. Régine liked the photo. It was her favorite picture of herself. The secret it contained made her smile every time she saw it. She looked forward to the second visit to Monsieur Dietens' photo studio, when the underside of the yellow star would be revealed to all.

Chapter Seven

WITHOUT SCHOOL, Régine spent most of her days in the apartment. The walls of the living room were covered with family photographs. She got to know them well from staring at them so much. There was her Aunt Ida, her father's sister, who lived in Brussels, only twenty minutes away by tram. She used to invite Régine for a dinner of roast beef on Sundays. Roast beef was something her mother never made, saying it was a luxury that "only Tante Ida can afford."

Then there was her favorite uncle, Zigmund, her father's brother who had gone from Poland to live in Germany first but left and came to Belgium when Hitler and the Nazis made life dangerous for Jews. When he still lived in Germany Oncle Zigmund had come to Brussels for a visit and brought Régine a doll as a gift. It was her one and only doll.

She stared at the picture of Oncle Shlomo and wondered what it was like in England now. When she was four, the family traveled to England by ferry on a visit and Oncle Shlomo taught her how to count to ten in English, the first English she ever learned. On the radio she heard that the Germans were bombing England. Was Oncle Shlomo all right?

The biggest photo hung above the bed in her parents' room. It was black and white in a heavy, wooden frame. It showed a young, handsome couple, the groom thin and good-looking in a dark suit, standing next to his bride who looked very pretty in her long white gown. Régine's parents had married in Poland in 1923. They came to Belgium in 1928 with Léon, who was two years old.

Régine was struck by how much her father still looked like the handsome man in the picture. Only her mother had changed. She looked too old and thin now to be the person in the picture. She also looked sadder. Régine knew the reason as she looked at her mother in the bed beneath the photograph. She was getting sicker all the time and got up for short periods at a time, then had to go back to rest.

Her father no longer took Régine to the Solidarité meetings. Acts of sabotage increased against war factories and communication lines. It was very dangerous. Suspects were rounded up and taken to the headquarters of the Gestapo, the German secret police. There they were shot and their names published in the newspapers for everyone to see, as a warning to anyone who thought of opposing the German occupation.

But the Germans killed not only suspected saboteurs. Anyone thought to be communist or socialist was an enemy of the Nazis. Many were taken away, never to be seen again.

One of the first to disappear was Monsieur Demers, the upstairs neighbor who used to invite her father to listen to his radio. Even though he was not Jewish, he had been arrested as a member of a Belgian organization opposing the Germans.

Régine often thought about the red underside of her Star of David. If anyone were to find out about it, what would happen? Her father was in danger, too. Her mother brought it up every time her father left the apartment. "Be careful," she whispered. "If they find out you're a member of Solidarité, you will be taken away like your friends."

"Don't worry," her father always answered. "They won't find out."

Few visitors now came to the apartment on rue Van Lint.

Not even Edgar Herman, her father's best friend and also a member of Solidarité. He used to drop in regularly and Régine missed his visits, even though whenever he came, she had to guard his bicycle downstairs, because Léon's bicycle had been stolen from that very spot.

When the Germans closed down Jewish businesses, including the leather companies, there was no work for her father. He found a new occupation. He took off his yellow badge and traveled by train to the countryside to get meat and smuggle it into the city. Not only could he be arrested for carrying the contraband meat, but also for riding the train, since Jews were forbidden to do so by the Germans. On the days he went to the country, Régine would go to the corner of rue Van Lint and Chaussée de Mons in the late afternoon and wait anxiously for his return.

He transformed his workroom into a butcher shop. His worktable became a butcher block and he sliced beef on it. Régine and Léon helped to wrap the meat for the women who came to buy it. Dr. Zilbershatz said her mother should have meat and her father was glad to provide it. But she had trouble digesting it and Régine often heard her vomiting in the bedroom.

Chapter Eight

THAT SUMMER, the terrible summer of 1942, the more the Allied bombers flew over Belgium, the worse the German orders against the Jewish people.

The deportations had started in March. Unmarried men between the ages of sixteen and forty were singled out for the labor camps. They were to be put to work erecting German fortifications along the northern coast of occupied France.

Léon was sixteen years old.

The knock came early one morning. Her father answered it. Her mother was resting in bed. At first it didn't seem too serious. The person at the door was a young man. He said he'd been sent to deliver a message to Léon Miller.

The young man was around Léon's age. He seemed nervous standing in her father's shadow. Léon leaned over and whispered in Régine's ear. "I know that guy. He went to my school."

"Is he your friend?" Régine asked.

"No, but I know him."

The young man handed the envelope to her father and turned to leave.

"Hold on," her father said. "What's this about?" He opened the envelope, took out the paper and unfolded it.

Régine saw the look of anger spread over her father's face. The young man, more nervous now, turned to go. Her father crumpled the paper and let it drop to the floor. He shoved the young man, and Régine heard him yell out as he tumbled down the stairs. Her father picked up the crumpled ball of paper and threw it down after him.

"What's going on?" her mother called in a weak voice from the bedroom. "Is something wrong?"

Her father slammed the front door and marched into the bedroom. She heard him say that Léon had to report to the train station in the morning. "We'll ignore the notice," he said.

"How can we ignore it?" her mother asked.

Her father did not answer.

A little while later there was another knock on the door. The same young man handed Mr. Miller another notice and ran quickly back down the stairs. Régine's father closed the door slowly, reading the new notice.

Her father again walked into the bedroom, followed by Léon. Through the open door Régine saw her father and brother sit down on the edge of the bed. Her father explained the notice to her mother. "Léon must go to the train station," he said, his voice a whisper.

There was no choice in the matter. If Léon didn't go, the whole family would be taken away.

Chapter Nine

RÉGINE WATCHED as her mother slowly packed Léon's rucksack. Piles of sweaters, pants and blankets lay on the bed. Mrs. Miller folded each item with precision and placed it in the bag. Her movements were painfully slow and deliberate. As Régine saw her mother sit down on the edge of the bed to rest, she wondered how her mother would survive the long walk to the train station.

"You don't have to come, you know, Mama."

"Of course I have to come," her mother said.

"Papa and I will take him."

"Yes, and I'm coming with you," her mother said. "I've already told you and it's settled."

Régine watched her mother pack the last sweater. The bag bulged and she struggled with the buckles to close it. Then she took hold of the shoulder straps, pulled the bag off the bed and dragged it along the floor into the other room.

Her father and brother were sitting on the sofa. They had been speaking in whispers. From the bedroom door, Régine could not hear what they were saying. Her father was doing all the talking. Was he telling Léon the war would end soon and they would all be back together?

They rose from the sofa as they saw Mrs. Miller with the heavy bag. Léon hurried to take it from her.

"You don't have to come," he told her. "Papa and Régine will accompany me. Really, Mama."

"But I want to come," Régine heard her mother say.

They left the apartment in silence. Régine and her father helped her mother down the stairs. They stood on either side of her, holding her by the elbows, and supported her on the long, slow walk to the train station, la Gare du Midi.

Along the way they stopped to rest from time to time. Régine wondered what she would tell Léon at the train station when it came time to say good-bye. It was hard to know the right thing to say.

She imagined herself at the station, standing on the platform. She saw herself kissing Léon on the cheeks and hugging him. Then he would board the train and, as it began to roll, she imagined him waving at her through the window.

She repeated this scene over and over in her mind as they walked toward the station. She only hoped that the right words would come to her on the station platform.

They were getting closer. Just a few more streets and around the corner and la Gare du Midi would be visible. Régine tightened her hold on her mother, who was tired now and dragging her feet.

The streets showed few signs that a war was going on. In Brussels, there were no bombed-out buildings or craters in the ground. The shops and homes stood where they had always stood. But the streets were usually quiet. Now they were busy with other families walking toward the train station, accompanying men with rucksacks on their backs.

A group of German soldiers passed. Régine was accustomed by now to seeing them on the street. They marched in pairs or in groups and wore helmets and uniforms and boots and carried guns or bayonets. Sometimes they rode military vehicles. But as far as she could see, they had no one to fight. Where were all the Allied troops that her father said would come to end the war and give Belgium back to the Belgians?

They turned the corner and saw the train station in the distance. A crowd had gathered in front. Something was going on, some kind of commotion. Her parents and Léon saw it, too, and stopped in their tracks.

Her father said, "Shhh! Listen!"

Régine heard the noise from up ahead, a mixture of shouts and screams, as if some shouted over the screams of others. She did not know what to make of it. She looked at her brother and saw from his face that he did not know, either. She tightened her hold on her mother's elbow.

"Come on," her father said.

The noise ahead of them grew louder. Soon they reached the front of the station. Régine saw now what was causing the commotion.

People were trying to enter the station and were being stopped. Men and women were pushing and yelling as they tried to pass through the front gate. Only the men carrying rucksacks on their backs were being allowed in.

Régine stood on tiptoe. The German soldiers swung their clubs and jabbed their bayonets to beat back the crowd. Their shouts could be heard over the screams.

A sudden jolt from behind almost caused her to fall over. She held firmly onto her father, who was supporting her mother. Two soldiers pushed their way through the crowd, and came toward them. In the confusion, she realized they were pulling her brother away. She must say good-bye, but she couldn't remember what she had planned. She grabbed his arm and she blurted out the only thing she could think of: "Don't work too hard for the Germans." It sounded like a joke and she regretted it. Then he was gone, a prisoner of the two soldiers, as they pushed him through the crowd toward the front gate. Her parents stood dazed beside her.

Her mother broke into sobs, burying her face in her

husband's chest. They had not been able to say good-bye to Léon at all.

All around people screamed and shouted as the soldiers continued separating men from their relatives and pushing them into the station. They swung clubs to keep the crowd away from the entrance. Régine thought she saw her brother's head among those going in, but she wasn't sure. There would be no final embraces on the station platform.

She took her place beside her mother, her father on the other side. Together the three began the long, slow walk home. Each time they would stop to rest her mother gave a choking sob. They could still hear the soldiers off in the distance shouting:

"Raus! Raus! Juden Raus!"

Chapter Ten

A FEW DAYS LATER Régine was sent away to a summer camp run by Solidarité. She should have enjoyed it, but thoughts of her brother came back, not just at night before she went to sleep, but even in the daytime when she tried to laugh with the others.

When Régine came home from camp a month later, her mother was back in the hospital.

Régine remembered the first time her mother entered the hospital. It was the only time she ever saw her father cry. Régine had visited her every afternoon after school with her father and brother, and the three of them stayed until the nurses told them to leave.

Régine had sat on the edge of her mother's bed and told her everything she was learning in school. Mademoiselle Descotte, her teacher, had shown the class how to knit, and Régine promised to teach her mother when she came back home.

Régine kept her promise. She showed her mother how to knit. Léon, too, wanted to learn, and the three of them knitted a long scarf. But her mother had changed. She had even less energy. She took the medicine from the bottles that bore a skull and crossbones on their labels and every few months she returned to the hospital for injections that left her covered with bruises.

Now back from camp and again standing at her bedside in the hospital, Régine was shocked to see how much thinner her mother had become. The hand held out to her seemed only bones, not at all like the strong hands that had ground nuts and stretched dough over the tabletop. Her mother tried to smile at Régine but the pain came through in her mother's voice as she spoke: "I'm sorry you have to see me like this."

Her father stood by in silence and remained silent during the walk home. That evening Régine found out why.

Her father sat Régine down on the sofa in the flat and sat down beside her. "I have something important to tell you," he began. He looked more nervous than she had ever seen him. "You know Monsieur Gaspar, don't you?"

Monsieur Gaspar was the father of Jeanne Demers, the upstairs neighbor whose husband had been taken away by the Germans. She had moved out but her father had stayed on. He and Régine's father always stopped to talk when they met on the stair landing.

"I was speaking with him just this morning," her father said. "He said maybe we should get some help."

"Yes?"

"He said we should find someone who will take care of you. Just for a little while. I think it's a good idea."

Régine frowned. "You mean Madame Sadowski?" Régine Sadowski was a family friend. But the last time she had helped while Mrs. Miller was in the hospital, she mixed the separate dishes kept for meat and dairy. Régine's mother had been very upset when she came home.

"No, no," her father said. "Monsieur Gaspar told me about someone else. Another woman. You will stay at her house."

"At her house?"

"Yes. Just for a little while."

"Who is she?" Régine asked.

"She's very old," said her father. "Her name is Madame André, and she lives alone in Boitsfort."

Boitsfort was a suburb of Brussels, and Régine thought it must be far because you had to take more than one tram to get there.

"Must I go, Papa?" she asked.

"Yes," her father said. "It's best this way."

"What about you?" Régine asked.

"I have work to do here. Your mother is safe in the hospital. And you will be safe in Boitsfort. All the arrangements are made." It was clear from his tone of voice that he did not want to explain any further. "I'll take you there in the morning."

This was unbearable. First her brother had been taken away, then her mother was taken to the hospital, and now to be separated from her father. He must have seen the look in her eyes.

"It will only be for a little while. She will take good care of you. And you can keep her company. She's very old. Monsieur Gaspar told me she's seventy-eight."

"Will you visit?" Régine asked.

"Every week," he said. "I promise."

They went into the bedroom to pack. Her father worked quickly. He pulled a duffel bag out of a closet and picked among her clothes. As he threw them on the bed, Régine noticed that none of the clothes he chose bore the yellow Star of David.

"Don't I have to wear the star?" she asked.

"No," her father said, angrily.

Régine understood now why her father was sending her away, why he wanted her to go live with a stranger. It had nothing to do with her mother's illness. That was just an excuse. It had to do with what had happened at la Gare du Midi.

The Germans had taken Léon away. Did her father fear she might be next?

Chapter Eleven

THEY LEFT the apartment the next morning. Régine carried her bag downstairs and waited at the bottom while her father locked the door. His fedora was tilted low over his forehead but it did not hide the worry in his eyes. Régine watched him come down the stairs. She noticed he also wasn't wearing the yellow star on his gray overcoat, just as when he went to the countryside to get meat.

They stepped out into the cobblestone street, still deserted only a few minutes after the nightly curfew was lifted. They walked toward the tram stop in silence, and Régine wondered when she would return to rue Van Lint. The future now frightened her. Her father had said he would visit every week. That meant she could be away for months.

They boarded the tram in silence and, even though they were the only passengers, they did not speak during the ride to Boitsfort. Régine glanced at her father but he did not look at her. She looked at the empty seats and wondered about the woman she was going to stay with. Madame André. She said the name over and over. It had a round, jocular ring to it. Perhaps Madame André would be fun-loving.

They changed trams, still without speaking. Régine tried to imagine Madame André sitting on an empty seat across from her. She saw a slight, elderly woman whose eyes lit up at the sight of children. Perhaps she wanted someone to talk to.

The tram entered the suburb of Boitsfort. Régine pressed

her face against the window and saw pretty houses with neat front yards and large trees. In the yards flower gardens were in full bloom. Régine had never seen so many bright colors. In Brussels, every building was attached to another and there was no space in between for grass to grow. But here, green was everywhere.

"This is our stop," said her father, getting up.

He picked up the duffel bag and Régine followed him to the door of the tram. Once her feet touched the sidewalk, the first thing she noticed was the freshness in the air. The sun was already shining and the air was warm. She took a deep breath to calm down. She was very nervous about meeting Madame André. The streets were strangely empty, however. Régine noticed there were no cobblestones. In Boitsfort, the streets were paved.

Her father pulled a piece of paper from his coat pocket and studied it. "This way," he said.

They passed several houses before stopping again so that her father could take another look at his piece of paper. Now they stood in front of a two-story house painted all in white. The front yard was enclosed by a low, brown fence and had a garden with red and yellow flowers.

Her father checked the number and put away the piece of paper. "This is it," he said, straightening his hat.

He pushed open the gate. Régine felt even more nervous as she followed him up the walk to the front door.

Before her father could knock, the door opened. Standing behind it was a heavyset woman, her white hair tied in a bun. She was so big, she almost filled the door frame. She didn't say a word, but just looked them over with a severe expression. The real Madame André looked nothing like the frail little woman Régine had imagined on the tram. She did not even look friendly.

"I am Miller," her father said.

"Come in quick!" Madame André said and stepped back to let them in. Régine saw her look nervously up and down the road before locking the door.

She was no more talkative inside the house than she had been in greeting them at the door. She did not ask any questions or invite her father to take off his coat. The three of them stood inside in silence. The woman was waiting for something. Régine's father reached into his coat pocket, pulled out an envelope and handed it to Madame André. Without comment, she took it, looked inside and nodded. Then she turned to Régine. "I'll show you your room."

Régine looked up at her father but did not know what to say. She did not want him to leave.

"I'll be back next week," he told her. "Promise."

They embraced, and Régine kissed him on the cheeks. Fighting back tears, she followed Madame André up the stairs.

Chapter Twelve

FOR THE FIRST TIME in her life Régine had her own bedroom. It had a dresser and a night table with a lamp. From the window she could see the tops of trees and roofs and into some of the windows of neighboring homes. The bed looked huge to Régine compared to the crib she had slept in all of her ten years. She unpacked and lay down, stretching out her legs. She tried to feel happy about the bed, the nice room and the one downstairs she had passed on her way up. It was lined with books. Léon would have liked that.

Régine had heard her parents say many times that they wanted their children to be well read. Léon was the biggest reader in the house. Hardly had he finished a book before he was back from the library with another one. His favorite was the French translation of *Ivanhoe* by Sir Walter Scott. "The best author," he told Régine.

One night while Léon was out with his friends, she had picked up the copy of *Ivanhoe* from the coffee table near the sofa and began to read. The words were harder than those in her school books, but she struggled with it until she reached the place where her brother had marked the page. Then she put the book back in the place where she had found it so that Léon would never know that she had been reading his book. Léon would not want her to touch anything of his.

She remembered how often she listened for the front door to unlock as she lay in her crib, and watched the crack of light shining beneath the door and imagined her brother preparing his bed on the sofa. She would wait for the light to go out again, listen to the faint shuffling of pages being turned in the other room. Her eyes would grow heavy but she forced them to stay open. She would stay awake until her brother went to sleep. Finally, the light went off, and Régine would close her eyes, thinking she would read the same pages the next day.

It had been the same every time Léon brought a book home from the library. Whatever her brother read, Régine wanted to read. Whatever he did, she had wanted to do. She read his favorite authors, listened to his favorite music and ate his favorite food. How excited he would have been to see the room full of books downstairs in Madame André's house. She tried to look forward to the new books she could read, but thinking about her brother made her feel sad again. Where was he? Was he all right? What was he doing? And what about his friends? Where was Léon Saktreger? Had he been taken away too? Were the Germans trying to send all the Jews away?

Chapter Thirteen

LATER THAT DAY, Madame André showed Régine the rest of the house. Her bedroom was upstairs, too, and next to it was a bathroom with a tub. It was the first time Régine had been in a house with a real bathroom. There was no bathroom in the Millers' building. The toilet in the hall was shared with the families who lived upstairs. It had a sink but no tub or shower. Like the other tenants, the Millers went to the public baths nearby, carrying their towels to save money. Régine bathed with her mother and Léon with his father. Whoever finished first waited for the others on the bench outside, and the family walked home together.

Unlike the apartment at rue Van Lint, Madame André's house had a separate dining room and kitchen. The window of the library looked out onto the front yard. The kitchen had something familiar to Régine: a big, wooden radio with short legs and large dials.

That night, the small supper showed Régine that food here was as scarce as it was back in the city. By now she was used to leaving the table still hungry. This was not going to change.

After supper they listened to Radio Free London, the same station Régine's father had listened to at home and in the Demers' apartment upstairs. He had explained that Radio Free London was the only station you could trust to give true accounts of the war because the radio stations in occupied

Belgium and France carried nothing but German propaganda. Radio Free London carried a program called *Les Français parlent aux Français*. It always ended with a message of hope and encouragement from the announcer. His words echoed in the house as Régine climbed the stairs to go to bed: *"Bonsoir et courage. On les aura les Boches!"* — Good night and courage. We'll get those Germans!

The next day, Régine asked whether she could leave the house to walk outside. Madame André refused. "Someone might see you," she said severely. "No one must know you are here."

Régine spent the next six days helping about the house. Madame André knitted baby dresses for extra money. She was pleased that Régine knew how to knit and got her started almost immediately on making sleeves for the little dresses. Régine also helped sew up the hems. She learned how to pin the dress to her own skirt so it would stay in place while she hemmed.

They worked together in almost total silence. Madame André did not act any friendlier as time passed. Each day seemed longer than the one before for Régine. It was not that Madame André was mean; she simply made no effort to be nice. Not once that week did Régine see a smile on her face.

The André house had another advantage, in addition to the nice room and bed and the library. Boitsfort did not have air-raid alarms. Madame André pulled the drapes at night but there was no taping of the windows. But Régine would gladly give up all those comforts to be back with her family.

Sunday finally came. The house was still dark when Régine jumped out of bed. She was so eager to see her father, she could not sleep. She had many questions to ask him. Was her mother still in the hospital? Was she feeling any better? And Léon? Had her father heard from him? Where was he?

What was he doing? Then the big question she would ask: might she come home soon? How about if she just went home with him now?

Régine got dressed, ran down the stairs and headed straight for the library. She sat down in a big armchair near the window and stared at the empty road out front.

"What are you doing down here at this hour?" a voice called out.

Régine turned and saw Madame André on the stairs in her housecoat. Her eyes were puffy with sleep. "Waiting for Papa," she said.

"But you don't even know what time he'll come!"

Régine shrugged. She knew he would come soon.

"You might wait for hours!" Madame André said. "He might not even come today. Maybe only tomorrow."

"He said one week."

"Yes, but he did not say Sunday."

"He said one week," Régine repeated. "He promised."

Madame André let out a sigh, turned and went back to her room.

Régine looked out at the empty road. When she went into the library on other days, it was to choose a book to read. But now she did not even glance at the shelves.

Hours passed. Régine sat in the chair all morning but saw no sign of her father. For a second she thought she had spotted him in the distance. A lone person was approaching. She craned her neck to get a better view. But it was not her father, and her shoulders sagged in disappointment.

More time passed. She heard the clanging of pots and pans in the kitchen and took this to mean that Madame André was preparing to bake. The sun was directly above the house and felt hot on her face as it shone through the window. It was early afternoon.

That's when she spotted him. There was no mistaking him this time. As before, Régine saw a lone figure in the distance. She could not see his face because he was too far. It didn't matter. She could make out the fedora on his head.

"Papa is here!" she called out.

Madame André emerged from the kitchen and headed for the front door. Régine watched through the window as her father arrived at the gate in his gray overcoat, adjusted his hat and walked up to the front door. Régine jumped out of her chair, full of excitement. She heard Madame André open the front door and the sound of her father's voice.

Her excitement was short-lived.

As short as his visit.

Again Madame André did not invite her father into the house. She kept him standing just inside the front door and accepted a second envelope of money. She seemed very anxious for him to leave.

"Papa," Régine said, stepping around the big woman.

"There you are," said her father, bending down to give her a hug. "Is everything all right?"

"Yes."

"Are you sure?"

"Yes."

"Are you happy?"

"Yes," Régine lied, again.

Madame André reached for the door handle, making it clear that she wanted him to go.

"I'll be back next week," he told Régine.

"You're leaving already?"

"Yes, I have to go," he said, glancing at Madame André.

Régine did not want him to leave. She wanted to ask him about her mother and brother. But Madame André was opening the door now and there was no time.

"I'll see you next Sunday," her father said, with a little wave of his hand. "That's a promise."

Madame André quickly locked the door behind him.

Chapter Fourteen

ON THE SECOND SUNDAY, nothing changed. Régine waited all morning at the window, and her father arrived in the early afternoon. He stayed only long enough to hand Madame André another pay envelope before he promised to visit Régine again in one week.

The third Sunday was different. This time her father did not seem to care that Madame André already had her hand on the door handle. He pushed his way in and pulled Régine close. He had tears in his eyes and Régine asked him what was wrong.

"It's about Mama," he whispered. "She's very sick. Much sicker than before."

"How come?" Régine said in a loud voice. "Isn't the hospital helping her?"

"That's just it," her father said, trying to keep his voice down. "She's not at the hospital anymore. They've sent her home."

"What do you mean, Papa? If she's sick, why did they send her home?"

"They can't keep her anymore," he said. "They're not allowed to."

Régine lowered her eyes. She understood too well. Her mother was not allowed to be in hospital because she was Jewish.

"Can I come home?" she asked. "I want to see Mama."

"Not yet," her father said.

"When can I see her?"

"Soon," he said.

Her father gave her a hug and turned to leave. "I'll be back next Sunday."

Once again, Madame André locked the door the moment he stepped outside.

On the fourth Sunday, her father did not come.

That morning Régine was up early and took her regular place by the window. Hours passed with no sign of her father on the empty road. In the early afternoon, at the usual time, her heart jumped when she finally spotted a lone figure in the distance coming this way. As the man approached, she saw that he was not her father.

Régine hurried from her chair to the front door as Madame André emerged from the kitchen. The old woman opened the door and jumped back in surprise when she saw that the man was not Monsieur Miller. It was Oncle Zigmund. Régine had not seen him in a long time.

"Who are you?" asked Madame André, her voice filled with suspicion.

"I am the little girl's uncle," he said. "I have brought the money."

"Oh." Madame André let out her breath. "Come in quickly," she said, closing the door behind him.

Zigmund Miller reached into his coat pocket, pulled out an envelope and handed it to her. Once or twice he shot Régine a nervous glance, but avoided her eyes.

"Where is Papa?" asked Régine. Something was wrong.

Her Oncle Zigmund hesitated. "Papa could not come today," he said finally.

"Why not?" Régine asked, feeling afraid all of a sudden. "Where is he?"

"He couldn't come," her uncle said, then changed the subject. "What about you? Is everything all right with you?"

"Why couldn't he come?" said Régine.

Her uncle glanced at Madame André. "I can't tell you right now," he said.

"Will he come next week?" Régine asked.

Oncle Zigmund hesitated again. "Maybe."

On the fifth Sunday, neither her father nor Oncle Zigmund came. This time it was Tante Ida who knocked on the door and hugged Régine, asked her how she was, paid Madame André, and left.

On the sixth Sunday, no one came at all.

Chapter Fifteen

ON THE SEVENTH SUNDAY, Régine was still keeping vigil at the window even though she had not seen her father in a month. Madame André told her she was wasting her time, but Régine did not listen.

In the afternoon, a man pushed open the gate and walked up to the door.

It was Monsieur Gaspar, the friend who had told her father about Madame André. Why had he come? Madame André let him in, and the two went into the kitchen. Régine followed. The three of them sat at the table.

Monsieur Gaspar looked at Régine and said, "Don't you have something to do?"

Régine did not answer.

"It's all right," Madame André said. "She can stay."

Monsieur Gaspar shifted in his seat and again addressed Régine. "I have something to discuss with Madame André," he said.

Madame André turned to Régine. "Why don't you go upstairs?"

Régine folded her arms and shook her head.

Monsieur Gaspar tried again. "Does she speak Flemish?"

Madame André shook her head.

Monsieur Gaspar began speaking in Flemish.

But Régine did know a little Flemish. She had studied it for one year at the *école primaire* where it was taught as a second language. She knew how to read it quite well and was beginning to understand when people spoke it. This time she understood immediately.

Monsieur Gaspar spoke quickly, as if he wanted to get the news over with. *"Haar moeder en haar broer zijn niet meer."*

Régine froze in her chair. It couldn't be true. She could not have heard it right. For a few seconds, all went silent at the kitchen table. Madame André looked at Régine nervously, then back at Monsieur Gaspar. That's when Régine realized the words were true and the full meaning hit her. She let out a violent scream and ran out of the kitchen. She tripped as she ran up the stairs to her room, picked herself up and kept on running and screaming. When she got to her bedroom she slammed the door behind her and threw herself onto the bed. She buried her head in the pillow and her screams slowly turned to sobs.

During the next week she spent most of her time in her room. Madame André never came near her, except to call her for meals. She lay on the bed half asleep, half awake, sometimes going over the scene — seeing Monsieur Gaspar at the front door, following him into the kitchen, sitting at the table and hearing his words: *"Haar moeder en haar broer zijn niet meer."* — "Her mother and her brother are no more." No more what? No more alive? She tried to think of another meaning the words could have. But if they did not mean something terrible, why would he have said it in a language he didn't think she understood?

At other times, she would go over the last time she had seen her brother. She saw herself walking with her parents and Léon toward la Gare du Midi. She saw again the crowds, the commotion, the German soldiers. She saw herself in the crowd, watching Léon hunch under the weight of his rucksack as the soldiers hustled him into the station.

Sometimes the scene was exactly as it happened. Sometimes it changed as she followed Léon into the crowd as far as the soldiers let her. When she came back to where she had left her parents, she found only her father, alone and crying.

Sometimes she saw the soldiers drag one last person toward the front gate. They swung their clubs and pushed people aside to clear a path. The last person was not her brother but a woman who could barely walk. It was her mother.

She went over the kitchen scene again and again. How had her mother died? Was she sent home to die? Had her father sent her to Madame André's so she would not see her mother die? And what about her brother? How did they know? Had he protested being pushed around? Is that why the Germans killed him? She focused on the exact words of Monsieur Gaspar, and one question came to mind. He had said that her mother and brother were dead, but he said nothing about her father. That could only mean that he was still alive. Perhaps he was hiding somewhere. When it would be safe to come out, he would come back to get her. She clung to the thought with all her might:

Papa is alive. He will come back.

She imagined herself sitting at the window, gazing out at the empty street. A lone man would approach in the distance, his hands buried in the pockets of his gray overcoat. He would reach the front gate, adjust his fedora and walk up to the door. There would be a loud knock. Régine would jump out of the armchair, run to open the door and throw herself into his arms. Her father would finally come to take her home.

It was a dream that kept her going.

Chapter Sixteen

O N THE EIGHTH SUNDAY she was back at the window watching. No one came all afternoon and as it got dark she fell asleep in her chair. She was awakened by a knock. For a second she did not know where she was, then she ran to the door.

A woman was standing there. She looked familiar but Régine could not place her. The woman wore a jacket over her dress and carried a briefcase. She had blond hair. Régine tried to think of someone she knew who had blond hair, but no one came to mind.

Madame André came up behind her to the front door. "Yes?" she said.

"Are you Madame André?" asked the blond woman. There was something nice about her voice and the way she spoke.

Madame André nodded.

"I would like to speak to you," the blond woman said. "May I come in?"

"What is it?" Madame André was her usual suspicious self.

"It's about Régine," said the woman. Seeing Régine, she smiled: "Bonjour, Régine. I have come to see if you are all right."

Régine froze. How did this woman know her name? Who was she?

Now she spoke to Madame André. "I'm here to arrange matters."

Madame André stepped aside to let the woman in, then closed the door and led her into the kitchen. Régine followed, feeling she was repeating the scene of the previous Sunday. Except this woman seemed too cheerful to be the bearer of more bad news.

"My name is Nicole." She sat down, ignoring Madame André's severe look of disapproval. Régine watched from the kitchen door.

"Am I right to assume that no one is paying you now to keep her?" she asked.

Madame André pursed her lips and did not answer.

The visitor laid her briefcase flat on the table, opened the straps, reached inside and pulled out an envelope. She counted out some bills and passed them across the table.

Madame André looked at the money without touching it. "Who are you?" she asked.

"My name is Nicole." She reached into her briefcase and pulled out a slip of paper. "If you ever need to speak with me, call this number. They'll know how to reach me."

She passed the paper across the table. Madame André glanced at it before slipping it into the pocket of her apron along with the money.

"I will pay you from now on," the woman continued. "I've been asked to keep an eye on Régine during the time that she will be living here."

"How long will that be?" Madame André asked.

The woman turned her head and saw Régine listening in the doorway. "We'll discuss that another time," she said to Madame André.

She closed her briefcase and stood up to go. At the door

she bent down and spoke to Régine. Her voice was kind.

"I'll be back next month," she said. "It's a promise. *Es-tu heureuse?* Are you happy?"

Régine nodded, too scared and confused to say anything to this woman who spoke just like her father. A flood of questions came but it was too late. Nicole said good-bye and Madame André had closed the door behind her.

Régine's nod had been a lie. Régine was not at all happy living with Madame André. She had been with her two months with no end in sight. There were so many unanswered questions. How long would she stay here? What had happened to her mother and brother? Where was her father? What about Oncle Zigmund and Tante Ida? Why didn't they come?

And who was this woman who had come to pay Madame André? She had looked familiar when she bent down to speak to Régine and pushed the blond hair back from her face. Régine was sure she had seen her before. If only she could remember the time and place.

It came to her that night as she lay in bed. She suddenly remembered where she had seen Nicole before. What had confused her was the name: Nicole. It was not her real name. And the blond hair. It was not her real color.

Régine remembered sitting up on a table in an apartment, wearing new boots up to the knees. A woman bent over and told Régine how pretty she looked in them. It was a Solidarité meeting in Edgar Herman's apartment. She remembered him coming to tell her father about meetings, and later, as she got older, guarding his bicycle while he was inside her house. The woman with the blond hair was not named Nicole. She was Fela.

It all came back in a rush of memories and images. Régine knew why Fela had changed her name and dyed her hair. Fela was Jewish, like the other members of Solidarité, like her father. She was part of the resistance to the Germans, the Belgian underground. She had come to Boitsfort to check up on Régine and to pay Madame André.

Régine closed her eyes. She fell asleep, feeling that she had someone who would look after her until her father returned.

Chapter Seventeen

FELA — NICOLE — came on Sundays in the early afternoon. She stayed only long enough to pay Madame André and ask Régine how things were going, after which she disappeared for another month. As winter approached she brought a coat and some heavy sweaters to last Régine through the colder weather. Régine took this to mean that she would not be leaving Boitsfort anytime soon. Nicole was her only link to happier times in Brussels. She was careful never to call her Fela, even when Madame André was not in the room. To avoid causing problems, she always told her that she was happy, even though that was far from the truth.

One evening during dinner, a knock came at the front door. Régine saw by the look on Madame André's face that visitors were not expected. She went to the front door and, without opening it, shouted: "Who's there?"

From where she was sitting, Régine could not hear the answer. Soon Madame André came in and asked: "Do you know a Mademoiselle Descotte?"

Régine almost fell out of her chair. "Mademoiselle Descotte! She's my teacher!"

"Well, she's here," Madame André said sharply. "Did you tell her you were living here?"

"No! I haven't seen her in months!"

"Well, somehow she found out you were here. She wants to talk to you," Madame André said. "She's outside. She has

54

some books for you. Take them and tell her to go."

Régine hurried to the front door. When she opened it, she saw a smiling Mademoiselle Descotte.

"Hello!" she said. "Can I come in?"

"Yes," Régine said, stepping to the side and closing the door behind her teacher.

"I'm so happy to see you. I went to your house. Monsieur Gaspar told me you were here," Mademoiselle Descotte said. "It's been such a long time. School has started again and we miss you very much."

Madame André came out from the kitchen. She was not happy to see a stranger in her house. "You have some books?" she said. "You came to give them to Régine?"

"No," Mademoiselle Descotte said. "I came to give her some lessons."

Madame André was startled. "There is no room here," she said.

"We could use the library," Régine suggested.

Madame André shot her a stern look and turned coldly to the visitor. "Who sent you here?"

Mademoiselle Descotte smiled as if there could be no objection. "I am her teacher. Since she cannot come to the school, I have come to her."

Régine led Mademoiselle Descotte into the library, where they spent an hour working on French composition. When they finished, Régine accompanied her teacher to the tram stop without asking permission from Madame André. Mademoiselle Descotte said she would return for more lessons.

Over the next month, Mademoiselle Descotte came to the house twice a week and each time Madame André showed her disapproval.

"All she wants is to save your soul," she told Régine, "like all good Catholics."

Régine did not know what this meant and repeated it to Mademoiselle Descotte one day as they walked to the tram stop. As soon as she said it, she knew it was a mistake. Mademoiselle Descotte was hurt by the accusation even though it came from Madame André and not Régine. Mademoiselle Descotte was silent as she boarded the tram, and she never came again.

Afterwards, Régine resented Madame André more than ever and began to spend as much time as possible on her own. When the chores were done and if there was no knitting to finish, she closed herself in her room or in the library while Madame André listened to *Les Français parlent aux Français* on the radio in the kitchen.

The library was Régine's favorite place. Every night she picked a book from the shelf, settled into a leather chair and read until her eyes grew heavy with sleep. Sometimes she even took a book into her room and slept with it in her bed. That winter she read all eight volumes of *Les Misérables*.

It was a good story, but it had not been her first choice. Months earlier she had searched for a familiar title among the rows of books, arranged in alphabetical order. She found the "S" section and cocked her head to read the name of each author. She looked carefully but nowhere did she see the name of Walter Scott — her brother's favorite author.

As she read *Les Misérables* night after night, she often cried over the character of Jean Valjean. One evening she fell asleep wondering if her brother had read the book, too. In her dream, Léon came home after school and apologized to his parents for being late for supper. He had been to the library, he said, and had a copy of *Les Misérables* which he set down on the table near the sofa. Then he rushed through dinner and ran out the door to meet his friends. "Don't wait up for me!" he called, waving as he disappeared down the stairs. In her dream,

Régine cleared the table and helped her mother wash the dishes. Then she sat down on the divan, turned on the table lamp and read *Les Misérables*. Later, lying in her crib, she heard the sound of a latch being opened beyond the closed door of the bedroom. Then a stream of light appeared under the door. It was Léon. Léon had come home!

"What are you doing?" snapped Madame André.

Régine shook herself awake. She had fallen asleep in the leather chair, and her cheeks were wet with tears.

"Why are you crying?" Madame André said, spotting the book in her lap. "What are you reading?"

"*Les Misérables*," Régine said softly. "You know, about Jean Valjean."

Madame André marched across the room and took the book from Régine.

"I don't understand," she said, shaking her head. "You cry over Jean Valjean but you never shed a tear for your own family."

Régine said nothing as she went into her room. Her family was all she thought about, but she did not have to prove it to Madame André. She closed the door of her bedroom and leaned against it, looking across the room at her bed. Then began the game that she now played every night before getting into bed.

She positioned her feet so they were exactly side by side, each within a separate square on the parquet floor. She curled her toes because it was very important that they should not touch any lines.

She studied the floor ahead of her as if it were a map, and focused on the first square where her right foot would land. She swung back her arms, and threw herself forward, landing in the center of the square. With arms extended for balance, she teetered on her right foot. She curled her toes and looked down at the floor, making sure she had not stepped on any lines.

Now came the hard part. She focused on another square a little to the left. She swung her arms back, pushed off her right foot and flew through the air until her left foot landed on the second square. Again she extended her arms, curled her toes and looked down to make sure she had not stepped on any lines.

She leapt from square to square until she reached the bed. She must not step on any of the lines. If she did not step on the lines, it meant her father was still alive and would soon come back to get her.

Régine learned to curl her toes so that every time she played the game, she won. So tonight, as on other nights, there was no doubt in her mind, absolutely none at all. Her father would come back.

Chapter Eighteen

MADAME ANDRÉ kept a garden in the back of the house where she grew vegetables and flowers. Régine loved the garden. She had never worked in one before. She picked the red currants, watered the primroses and pulled the weeds. She wished her father could see her with her garden tools. *Papa would be proud.*

But she was not allowed to go out in the front of the house during daytime. Madame André was afraid of attracting attention. She took Régine out only in the evening, after dark, to deliver the baby clothes she made or to visit her sister who lived a few streets away.

Madame André remained unfriendly. She spoke little to Régine, and never about herself. At her sister's house, the two women did not include Régine in their conversation. Régine discovered that the old woman was a widow by peeking at the letters that came to the house addressed to *Madame Veuve André* — Mrs. Widow. She decided Madame André's late husband had been a writer because two books with the André name sat on the shelves in the library.

She also learned that Madame André had a son when a package arrived from him early one morning. The knock came at the front door as they were having their usual breakfast of bread, jam and coffee. The jam was made from red currants from the back garden, and the coffee was not coffee at all but a mixture of roasted malt and chicory which everyone called *ersatz*. With unusual excitement, Madame André bolted from her chair and rushed to answer the front door.

Régine went to the library window and pulled back the drapes. Parked out front was a military vehicle with a red cross on its hood. A man in uniform stood at the front door with a parcel under his arm. Madame André took it from him, closed the door, and returned to the kitchen.

Régine followed Madame André back to the kitchen and watched her tear the plain-brown wrapping and take out its contents: tins of sardines, bags of flour, figs, cookies and other foods that were hard to come by in wartime Belgium.

"It's from my son, Jean," Madame André announced. "He lives in Africa. In the Belgian Congo."

Régine had never seen Madame André so excited. It was the first time she had shown any pleasure.

Minutes later, another knock sounded at the front door. This time the visitor was a woman whom Régine had seen but never met. It was the next-door neighbor. Régine had noticed her beyond the hedges when she worked in the back garden but they had never spoken. The neighbor carried a carton of eggs into the kitchen, put it on the table and waited while Madame André poured some of the newly arrived flour into a bag. The Red Cross truck meant Madame André had received another parcel from her son and the neighbor wasted no time coming over to trade her eggs for flour.

She was much younger and considerably more petite than Madame André and also more pleasant. She turned to Régine and introduced herself. "I'm Madame Charles." She sounded friendly. "I've seen you working in the garden. If you ever want to give me a hand with my garden, you're always welcome. Come over anytime."

"Thank you," Régine said and looked at Madame André. The old woman did not object. "You're allowed to go to

60

Madame Charles's house, but nowhere else."

The two women must have discussed her. Madame Charles must know Régine was Jewish and could be trusted to keep the secret or Madame André would never let her go there.

"If you want to come today you can help me pick some red currants and make some jam."

Régine turned to Madame André. "May I?"

"Straight there and back. Understood?"

"Yes," Régine said.

That afternoon Régine and Madame Charles poured red currants into pots, added sugar and poured the jam into glass jars. They sealed the jars with squares of paper and elastic bands. Madame Charles did most of the talking and asked many questions. How old was she? Did she have any hobbies? What did she want to do when she was older? Had she ever traveled? Hungry for conversation after so many weeks, Régine told Madame Charles that she was ten years old and that her birthday was in March, that she loved to read and knit, and that she wanted to become a schoolteacher someday. She told her all about Mademoiselle Descotte, her teacher at the *école primaire* in Brussels who had come to give her lessons. As for traveling, she had traveled only once, to England for a visit to her Oncle Shlomo.

Régine was too shy to ask questions. She knew Madame Charles was married because her husband left for work each morning. They had no children, or their children were no longer living at home. Régine never saw anyone else at their house.

The jam-making sessions continued once a week throughout the late summer. Madame Charles continued to do most of the talking as if she wanted to make Régine feel comfortable. Sometimes Régine brought gooseberries from Madame

André's garden and in the early evening she was handed two full jars of jam. She liked the feel of the warm fruit jars in her hands as she carried them back to Madame André.

When she was not visiting Madame Charles, Régine helped Madame André at home with the housework: cleaning floors, dusting furniture, changing sheets and washing clothes. They made bread from the flour her son sent from Africa, and ate it at breakfast with the jam from next door. Régine helped knit the baby dresses and sometimes, after dark, Madame André took Régine with her to deliver them to her clients.

Chapter Nineteen

THE WAR WENT ON and on. March 16, 1943, arrived: Régine's eleventh birthday. A year ago she had been with her family. Now the best birthday present she could imagine would be if her father came to get her.

She climbed out of bed and crept to the window. From the second floor she could see over the tops of trees to the neighboring houses. The trees were already starting to bud. There was one house in particular that she always looked at because she could see inside the top window. That was where the boy lived.

She had seen him there for a week now. He looked about her age and had straight, auburn hair just like hers. The boy smiled shyly from his window. When Régine smiled back, she felt warm inside.

That was all. They never waved or mouthed any words to each other. The boy appeared only in the window, never in the yard or on the street. Every morning, just before seven o'clock, they looked across at each other from their windows. Then Régine went downstairs to join Madame André at the breakfast table.

That morning of her eleventh birthday, Régine was particularly grateful to see the mysterious boy. She continued to see him for another week. Then one morning he was not there. She waited for half an hour in case he was late but he did not appear. Régine did not know what to think. Had she offended him? Had he grown tired of seeing her?

"What are you doing at the window? Didn't you hear me call you to breakfast?" Madame André stood in the doorway of the bedroom. "What are you looking at?"

"Nothing," Régine said.

Madame André walked to the window. "What's so interesting outside?"

"Nothing."

"Then come downstairs."

Madame André walked out of the room. Régine followed. At the top of the stairs she turned, rushed back to her room and looked out the window once more.

Every morning in the days that followed, she continued to look for him but she never saw him again. She never knew his name or where he came from. She never mentioned him to anyone, not even to Madame Charles or Nicole. The secret would belong to her and the mysterious boy.

In later years she often thought about the boy. Maybe he did not live in that house and was not even a visiting relative of the family. Maybe the boy was Jewish. Maybe he too had been taken to a stranger's house to hide from the Germans. She never forgot him. He became yet another person who disappeared from her life.

One evening Madame André announced: "We're going to Brussels."

"To Brussels?" Régine asked.

"Yes. To deliver some dresses. A customer needs them right away."

Although Madame André took Régine out now and then when she went to deliver the baby clothes, this was the first time they would be going all the way to Brussels. Régine was frightened at the prospect. As usual, they waited for darkness before leaving the house. They walked to the tram stop, each carrying a box filled with the knitted baby dresses.

By the time they reached Brussels, it was pitch black outside. Régine squinted through the window and tried to make out the shops and buildings in the shadows. Was she close to rue Van Lint? Madame André tapped her on the shoulder, indicating it was time to get off.

Régine followed her to the exit carrying the box. She hopped onto the street and felt the familiar rough edges of the cobblestones under her feet. For a second she thought that maybe this was rue Van Lint. She looked around but did not recognize any of the buildings.

"This way," Madame André said.

They walked to a house a few blocks away, and Madame André rang the doorbell. Régine looked up and down the dark and empty street. She felt more scared now than when they left Boitsfort, and suddenly she was anxious to get back. She was so full of fear that she did not notice a dark figure coming suddenly out of the shadows and running straight toward them. The approaching stranger was a woman and she seemed to recognize Régine. But Régine was sure she had never seen this woman before. Madame André rang the doorbell over and over, desperately asking for the door to open.

The strange woman let out a scream and grabbed at Régine. Régine dropped the box of baby dresses and stood paralyzed as the woman threw her arms around her and began to sob hysterically. "They took my child! Where is my child! They took her! They took her!"

Régine tried to break free but the woman would not let go. Madame André grabbed Régine's arm and pulled. Just then the door to the house opened and a woman inside stared at the sight of the commotion.

"What's going on?"

Régine managed to free herself. She picked up her box of baby dresses from the ground and ran inside the house. Madame André followed her in and slammed the door, leaving the sobbing woman standing outside.

"They took my child! They took her! They took her!"

Régine could still hear her through the door. It was only then that she realized the woman was speaking in Yiddish.

"Who was that woman?" Madame André snapped.

"I don't know," Régine said.

"She seemed to know you," said the other woman, the customer.

"I have never seen her before in my life," Régine insisted, annoyed that they did not believe her when she was speaking the truth, and upset by the suffering of the strange woman.

Later that night she relived the episode in a nightmare and was awakened by the same scream. The only difference was that in the nightmare someone else was sobbing in Yiddish. Now the hysterical woman was no longer a total stranger. This time the woman was her mother.

Was it possible that she was a long-forgotten friend of her parents who recognized her? Or did Régine remind the woman of a child who had been taken away? There was no way of finding out.

Madame André was so shaken by the incident that she never again took Régine on another excursion. She seemed more determined than ever to keep her out of sight. She looked out the windows to make sure no one was watching before letting Régine even cross the yard to Madame Charles's. Radio reports of the war seemed to make her more nervous.

Régine knew that her stay in Boitsfort would soon come to an end.

Chapter Twenty

THAT END CAME on September 10, 1943. Nicole arrived as usual in the early afternoon for what Régine thought was her monthly visit. Instead it was her last. "Go upstairs and pack your bag," Nicole told her.

Nicole gave no explanation. None was necessary. Régine knew the reason: Madame André was scared of being caught by the Germans with a Jewish child in her house and had called Nicole to come and take her away.

Madame André had become more nervous with each passing day. The war showed no sign of letting up, and the news accounts on the radio were contradictory. Belgian radio spoke of German victories. Britain, they said, was on its knees now that London had been razed by German bombers. Régine wondered what had become of Oncle Shlomo and his family.

Régine had liked the broadcasts on Radio Free London, especially the strange messages — "codes," Madame André called them — about birds, and animals and the weather. It meant that someone in London was talking to someone in Belgium, helping to end the war. She also liked the British broadcasts because they contradicted Belgian radio. By the fall of 1943, Radio Free London was saying that Germany had surrendered in Russia and North Africa, and the Allies were going to free Italy. It was good to hear.

But in Belgium, nothing had changed and she had to move again.

Régine pulled her canvas bag out from under the bed and began to fill it. She walked to the window for the last time, looked out over the trees and roofs of neighboring homes, and imagined the boy smiling at her from the top window of one of the houses. Then she carried her bag downstairs.

The front door was open and Nicole was waiting for her at the gate. Madame André stood at the door. Régine did not know what to say and waited for Madame André to speak first. Maybe there would be a hug or even a kiss. There had never been any show of affection between them but now that she was leaving, perhaps. But Madame André did not even say good-bye. As Régine went down the steps, she heard the door shut behind her.

"Ready?" Nicole said.

"Ready," said Régine. She put down her bag and looked back at the house where she had lived for over a year.

"Where will I go?" she asked Nicole.

"To Uccle. Do you know where that is?"

Régine nodded. Uccle was another suburb of Brussels. They could reach it by tram.

"Where will I stay?"

"You will live with a family," Nicole said. "The Bernards. All the arrangements are made. They are hairdressers and work out of their home. They have a daughter. Plus another girl who is Jewish. So you'll have friends your own age. I think you'll be happy there."

"The people are Jewish?" asked Régine.

"No, no. Just the other girl who is visiting. She's a friend of the daughter. You can all become friends."

"How old are they, the girls?"

"A little older than you," Nicole said. "Maybe fourteen or fifteen."

She picked up her bag and followed Nicole through the gate. Then she heard a voice call her name. Régine turned and saw Madame Charles standing at her door, waving at her to come. Régine dropped her bag again and ran to say good-bye. She got not only a hug and a kiss, but also a warm jar of gooseberry jam.

Chapter Twenty-one

THE TALL, NARROW HOUSE stood on a quiet, tree-lined street that, like Boitsfort, seemed worlds away from the clutter and noise of Brussels. Régine's room was on the upper floor and again it had a view of neighboring homes. But now she shared the room with the two other girls Nicole had told her about.

Nicole had predicted that they could all be friends, and Régine hoped so, too. She looked forward to having other girls to talk to. But as soon as she walked into the room she had the feeling that Nicole was wrong. The beds of the two girls had been placed side by side at one end of the room while her own bed stood alone at the other end. It did not seem friendly at all. That night as she lay in her new bed, Régine heard the two girls whispering in the dark. They did not want to include her in their conversation.

The next day the girls went out on an errand.

"You're too young to come with us," the first girl said to Régine.

"And you have chores to do," said the second. The girls giggled and walked out the door.

Régine was left behind to make the beds.

In the days that followed Régine found herself being treated like a servant. She had to change sheets, dust furniture and scrub floors. By the end of the first week, her hands and knees were covered with calluses.

The hardest room to clean was where Monsieur and Madame Bernard worked. The room was at the back of the house and had two tall chairs and two sinks with mirrors above them. There was also a big hair dryer where women customers sat, reading magazines.

The floor was always covered with hair. No sooner had Régine swept it than she had to start all over again. Customers came and went all day. Régine was expected to stay out of sight when clients were in the house. But as soon as they left, tracking hair all the way to the front door, she was called in to sweep up.

As she swept and scrubbed, Régine felt the eyes of her father watching her. She doubted that he would approve of the work she was expected to do. But then again, she thought if he were here he would probably say it was necessary for the sake of Nicole who was doing her best to hide Régine from the Germans. She decided not to mention anything when Nicole visited after the first week.

"Are you happy?" Nicole asked, after handing over the pay envelope.

Régine lowered her eyes and uttered a weak "yes."

"Are you sure?"

"Yes," Régine repeated, hiding her despair.

"Good. I'll be back in a few weeks," Nicole told her.

Régine would have liked to rush after her, but instead she stood and watched. She wished that she was still in Boitsfort. Madame André had not been friendly but she was better than the Bernards. The two girls made Régine feel more lonely than when she had stayed with the solitary old woman.

She was particularly upset because of the Jewish girl. She had hoped to be her friend and wanted to ask her questions. Where was she from? Where were her parents? Why was she staying here? Was she hiding from the Germans, too? But the girl paid no attention to her.

One day, Madame Bernard announced a surprise.

"We're not expecting any customers today," she told Régine. "Why don't we do your hair? Would you like that?"

Régine nodded enthusiastically. She had often wished to change the style of her hair, which was straight and plain. Its auburn color was more red than brown. Adults had always admired the color, but the kids at school used to make fun of her and called her "*roussette*," or redhead.

Her hair had been kept short by her mother so it would be clean and shiny, but it had grown long during the year she had stayed with Madame André.

"How about a permanent?"

A permanent! It was exactly what she had always wished for. Curls!

Régine settled into one of the tall chairs, and Madame Bernard went to work. She tied a large bib around Régine's neck and washed her hair in the sink. Without cutting her hair, she began applying the permanent lotion and putting on the curlers. Then Régine was put under the big dryer.

It took an awfully long time for her hair to dry, or so it seemed to Régine, who was eager to see herself with curls. The dryer was turned off and Régine sat in the tall chair so the curlers could be removed. It seemed to take forever. Was something wrong?

"Almost finished," said Madame Bernard.

"How does it look?" Régine asked. She could not see because the mirror hung on the wall behind her.

"You have to give it some time. That's the way it is with a permanent. After a few days it will look nice."

When the last curler was removed Régine was handed a small mirror. She brought it up slowly and looked at her reflection. What she saw was worse than she could have imagined. She held the mirror at arm's length for a wider view but the sight did not improve. She brought her free hand up to her head and grabbed at her hair. The curls were so tight she could not run her hand through it.

"Don't worry," Madame Bernard said. "It'll get better." She looked pleased with herself.

But her hair did not get better. She still could not put a comb through it by the end of her first month when Nicole arrived. She reacted with shock when she saw Régine. She handed over a pay envelope and took Régine aside.

"What did they do to your hair?"

Régine lowered her eyes. She did not want to cause trouble for Nicole. Monsieur and Madame Bernard were standing right behind her.

"It's nothing," she began to say, but her voice cracked.

Nicole bent down and looked into her face. "What's wrong? Tell me."

"It's nothing."

"Is it your hair?" Nicole asked. "Don't worry. It's not that bad. It'll get better."

"It's not that," Régine said, and held out her hands.

Nicole took hold of Régine's hands and her eyes widened. Calluses covered her knuckles completely. The tips of her fingers were cracked and showed traces of dried blood. Her fingernails were broken. Nicole rose and stared at the Bernards. Régine had never seen her so angry.

"Go up to your room," Nicole told Régine. "I have some things to discuss here."

Régine climbed the stairs wondering if she had done the right thing. Would her father have approved? She sat on the edge of her bed and remembered what he had told her as he sat at his worktable and cut a square of red material into the shape of a star to glue on the back of the yellow Star of David the Germans were forcing them to wear.

"If you are forced to do something you think is wrong," her father had said, "then you must protest." Régine decided she had done the right thing by showing Nicole her hands.

A few days later, Nicole returned. She took Régine aside and told her she had made arrangements for her to stay with another family. That was not all. Nicole said she had something to tell her. She could not explain to her right away although it was very important.

"Go pack your bag," Nicole told her. "We don't have much time."

What important news did Nicole have for her? Was it about her father? Régine hurried up the stairs. She was relieved to be leaving this household after only one month. She returned downstairs and said a curt good-bye to Monsieur and Madame Bernard. They looked embarrassed.

Nicole was waiting outside. Régine went to join her, passing the two girls who stood watching. She heard them giggle just before the door slammed behind her.

Chapter Twenty-two

RÉGINE BOARDED THE TRAM and took a seat by the window with her duffel bag in her lap. She scratched her messy head and waited nervously for Nicole to tell her the important news.

Nicole held her briefcase tightly as she spoke. She had to talk fast, she said, because there was very little time. They were going to the bus station in Brussels. Régine would take a bus that would bring her to a new hiding place in the countryside.

"You understand? It won't be like before," she told Régine. "I won't be able to visit you. It will be too far."

Régine could not hide her disappointment. "You mean, I won't see you?"

"It is only for three months," Nicole said, "and I'll write."

"Where will I be living?"

"In Andoumont," Nicole said. She put her briefcase flat on her lap. "It's a small village in Liège."

Régine had never been to Liège but knew that it was south of Brussels, not far from the Ardennes mountains and the German border. She had learned by heart at the *école primaire* all the nine provinces of Belgium and their capital cities. The capital of the province of Liège was easy to remember because it was also called Liège.

Nicole rummaged inside her briefcase. "It's smaller than Boitsfort. And the people you'll be with live on a farm."

Many children from Brussels had been sent to live in the

countryside since the German occupation began more than three years before. The countryside was safer than the city in the case of bombings and food was more plentiful.

"These people have two children," Nicole said, still rummaging. "So you won't be alone. And you'll be going to school."

"To school?" Régine's eyes lit up at the prospect. "Really?"

"Yes," Nicole said, pulling out an envelope. She looked through the window and frowned. "We're almost there. We're very short of time, so you'll have to listen carefully."

She opened the envelope and pulled out a booklet of ration cards. This certainly could not be the important news. Régine had known about ration cards ever since the beginning of the war. The stamps inside were used for buying vegetables, eggs and milk and other foods that were rationed and hard to get. The booklet also served as identification. It showed the name, age and residence of the carrier. Nicole handed the booklet to Régine.

"This is yours," Nicole said.

Régine read the name printed on the booklet. It said Augusta Dubois.

"Who's that?" she asked.

"You," Nicole said.

"Me?"

"This is what I had to tell you," Nicole said. "From now on you are Augusta Dubois."

"But I'm Régine Miller."

"I know that," said Nicole. "But from now on no one else must know your real name. What I'm saying is: *Tell no one who you are*. Do you understand? This is very, very important."

Régine nodded, sensing the urgency in Nicole's voice again. "I understand."

76

"Good. You won't forget? You are Augusta Dubois, not Régine Miller."

"I won't forget. I'm Augusta Dubois."

"And you come from Marche, not Brussels."

"From Marche?" Régine knew that Marche was even farther south than Liège.

"Yes," Nicole said. "Your name is Augusta Dubois and you come from Marche. That's all you have to remember, but it's very important." She paused. "City children are being sent to live on farms. It's part of a program called *l'Aide paysanne aux enfants des villes*. Farm families care for children from the city for three months. Understand?"

Régine nodded. She understood very well. It was dangerous to be Jewish under the German occupation, and the name Augusta Dubois did not sound at all Jewish. Dubois was a safer name than Miller, just like Nicole was a safer name than Fela and blond hair was safer than dark.

"Is that why I can go to school?" Régine tried to look forward to the change.

"Yes. You will attend the same school as Marie, the daughter. They will make all the arrangements," Nicole said.

"How old is Marie?" asked Régine.

"She's nine, two years younger than you. She has an older brother, Jean, who is nineteen."

Nicole looked out the window. "There's the station," she said. "We're here."

Régine saw rows of buses, surrounded by a crowd of children and grownups. She slipped the ration book into her duffel bag and felt confused. How would she handle her new, secret identity? What awaited her in Andoumont? She stood up slowly and followed Nicole to the front of the tram.

"Hello," she said to herself, too softly for anyone else to hear. "I'm Augusta Dubois, and," she hesitated for a moment, "and — I come from Marche."

Nicole held Régine's hand and guided her through the crowd. The children were noisy and excited as they hugged their parents. They seemed to be happy to be going to the country, as if it were an adventure. Régine wished she felt the same.

At the end of a long row of buses Régine and Nicole reached one marked "Liège." The bus was almost full. At the door was a man wearing a ribbon marked *Aide paysanne* and Nicole introduced Augusta Dubois. The man looked at the sheet of paper and nodded: "You are going to Andoumont. Go ahead and get on. I will call your name when we get to your stop."

Nicole bent down and gave her a hug and kiss on the cheek. "Everything will be all right," she said. "Just don't forget what I've told you."

Régine dropped her duffel bag and hugged Nicole with all her might. Then she bent down and rummaged through her bag. She pulled out the jar of gooseberry jam that Madame Charles had given her a month before and presented it to Nicole just as the man called out: "Let's go!"

She picked up her duffel bag, gave Nicole a weak smile and climbed onto the bus.

"Don't forget!" called Nicole.

Régine moved down the bus until she found an empty seat by the window. She sat down with the duffel bag in her lap and looked around. She had not seen so many children in one place since she was forced to leave the *école primaire* more than a year before. The children pressed their faces against the windows and waved to their parents. Régine looked out to Nicole but did not dare to wave.

The bus began to move. Régine craned her neck and

watched Nicole standing on the sidewalk with her briefcase in one hand and the jar of gooseberry jam in the other. She did not move, even after most of the other grownups had begun to walk away. She stood there for as long as Régine could see her.

During the long ride to the countryside, Régine studied the other children on the bus. If they were as afraid as she was, they did not show it. Or were they noisy to mask their fear? Every few miles the bus came to a stop and the man from *Aide paysanne* called out the name of the village and of the children who were to get off.

She now saw a boy sitting across the aisle farther toward the back. She had not noticed him before in the midst of all the noise. He was as quiet as she was. He had red, curly hair and she wished that her permanent had turned into nice curls like his instead of leaving her hair full of knots which she always felt like scratching.

The boy seemed shy. Every time he caught her looking at him, he turned away. He reminded her of the boy in the window when she was living with Madame André. That boy had been shy, too. He never spoke or waved during their secret through-the-window meetings. Even his smiles were guarded, as if they hid an important truth.

The more she peered at him, the more she felt there was something that set him apart from the children around him. It was the look in his eyes. It showed fear, confusion, anger and apprehension — the same emotions she was feeling. Yes, Régine thought, the boy must be Jewish.

"Andoumont!" the *Aide paysanne* man called out from the front of the bus, then added a list of names.

Régine placed the duffel bag in the empty seat beside her and stood up. She straightened her coat, picked up her bag and walked past the boy with the curly, red hair. She caught him looking at her and wondered whether he had guessed her secret, too. Was it so evident? Would others be able to see through her?

She stepped off the bus as Nicole's strange words echoed again in her head: "*Tell no one who you are.*"

Chapter Twenty-three

ABOUT A DOZEN PEOPLE had gathered at the village terminal to greet the bus as it arrived in Andoumont. The station was little more than a signpost on a stretch of dirt road, nothing like the crowded terminal in Brussels. Régine got off with five other children and then she hesitated. She had no idea what the people meeting her looked like.

The *Aide paysanne* man began to call out names. One by one the children stepped forward and were met by their designated hosts. Régine stood waiting for her name to be called. As the others walked away in pairs or small groups, she was left beside the *Aide paysanne* man.

"Are you Augusta?" he asked.

"Pardon?"

"I said, are you Augusta Dubois?"

"Yes, yes," she answered nervously. "Augusta Dubois. I come from Marche."

"Why didn't you answer when your name was called?" The question came from a young man who had been standing nearby

"Sorry," Régine said softly. "I guess I didn't hear."

"Well I heard and I was further away than you." He sounded angry. "I'm Jean," he said briskly. "My parents sent me to get you. Let's get going."

Régine picked up her duffel bag and followed Jean along the dirt road. She told herself to be more attentive the next time, and quicker in answering if she did not want to give everything away.

The dirt road led through dark green pastures and tall fields of wheat. Régine had never seen so much open space in her life. The farms around Andoumont made places like Boitsfort and Uccle seem like cities. As for Brussels, well, it did not belong in the same world.

Not a word was spoken as they walked, but all along the way Régine felt the eyes of Jean studying her. Finally he pointed to a farm up ahead and said: "That's where we live."

The family farm was even bigger than she had imagined a farm to be. Fields of wheat stretched out from behind the farmhouse as far as she could see. On one side of the house, cows grazed in an open pasture. On the other side, next to the barn, a tractor stood idle. Régine followed Jean along a footpath that led from the dirt road up to the front of the house.

She was met on the porch by Monsieur and Madame Carpentier and their daughter, nine- year-old Marie. The first thing Régine noticed was that Monsieur Carpentier was as tall as his son, while Madame Carpentier was as short as her daughter.

Madame Carpentier was very cheerful. "Come in, come in!" she said. "Jean will take your bag upstairs. Did you have a good trip? We were so anxious for your arrival."

Madame Carpentier took hold of her elbow and led her inside the house. Her husband and Marie followed.

"When you put your things away, we have a nice surprise for you!" Madame Carpentier said.

"A surprise?" Régine asked.

"Yes. There's someone we want you to meet!"

Jean took her to an upstairs bedroom, dumped her duffel bag inside the door and left without saying a word. He did not seem happy about having her here. There was another bed in the room and Régine realized, judging from the doll on it, that she would be sharing the room with Marie. She wished Marie would appear so she could ask who it was she would be meeting. Who could it possibly be?

Later that afternoon she was led into the living room, where an elderly couple sat, smiling. She had never seen them before. Why would they want to meet me? she wondered.

"These are Monsieur and Madame Lalonde, our neighbors," Madame Carpentier said. "They rushed over as soon as they heard you were coming."

"Bonjour!" said the elderly couple in unison.

"Bonjour," she said slowly.

"The Lalondes have been our friends for a long time," Madame Carpentier continued. "They live on the next farm. And they have relatives in Marche."

Régine shrugged. What difference did it make where these people came from? Monsieur Lalonde's smile broadened. He seemed about to speak when Madame Carpentier jumped in again.

"Marche!" she announced. "Just like you! Their relatives might know your parents. Can you believe it?"

Madame Carpentier dragged a chair to the middle of the room for Régine to sit on. Then she turned and sat on a chair beside her husband and Marie. Jean came down and leaned against the wall, watching. Régine sat in the chair in the middle of the room and felt she was on display.

"What a small world we live in!" Madame Carpentier said, clutching her heart as if the thought of it was too much for her.

"Yes, it's true," Monsieur Lalonde said, turning to Régine. "Tell us, where in Marche do you live?"

Régine had never been to Marche in her life. Not only that, Monsieur Lalonde spoke Walloon, a dialect of French that Régine did not understand. The Lalondes must have sensed this and they switched to French.

"What street do your parents live on?" Madame Lalonde asked.

"We know lots of people in Marche," said her husband. "What does your father do?"

Régine tried to think how to answer. But there was no way. She swung her legs and stared at the floor. Her only hope, she decided, was to say nothing. That's it, she told herself, just play dumb.

"Is something wrong?" Madame Carpentier asked.

"She's shy," Madame Lalonde suggested.

"Are you shy, Augusta?" asked Madame Carpentier.

Régine nodded.

"I don't think she's shy," Jean said, still leaning against the wall. "I think she's stupid."

"Jean!" his mother objected.

"She didn't even answer when her name was called at the bus stop! She doesn't know her own name!"

"Maybe she didn't hear it," Madame Carpentier said.

"Well, she can hear us now," Jean said. "So why is she just sitting there?"

Why does he hate me so much? Régine wondered. She felt scared, embarrassed and angry: scared that they would find out her secret, embarrassed about having to pretend to be stupid, and angry at Nicole for getting her into this mess.

It was not her fault that she could not answer their questions. Nicole had told her nothing about Augusta Dubois. Régine did not even know whether such a person existed. Was her new name borrowed from someone else, or just invented?

She looked up from her chair and saw that everyone was watching her, waiting for her to say something. She braced herself for more questions. Jean leaned forward, ready to pounce.

Madame Carpentier sighed, as if she were disappointed. Then she said, "Take Augusta upstairs, Marie, and show her your dolls and books."

Régine breathed a sigh of relief. She hopped off the chair and followed the girl upstairs.

Régine could not sleep that night as the events of the day played over in her mind. She lay on her back and stared into the darkness while Marie slept soundly in the bed next to hers. She thought about Nicole and ground her teeth in silent rage.

It was not enough to say "I am Augusta Dubois and I come from Marche." If other people were to believe her, she needed more than that. She needed a ready lie for every question they might ask. Since she couldn't fall asleep, she turned over on her stomach and began to make up a story about Augusta Dubois.

It was necessary to think things over very carefully.

Problem Number One: She knew nothing about Marche. So the best solution was to say she no longer lived there. She could say that she had moved away after the German invasion of Belgium. That was in May 1940, three and a half years ago, so it made sense that she did not remember much about her home town of Marche.

Problem Number Two: Where had she been living all this time? Régine closed her eyes and imagined the house in Boitsfort. She had lived there with Madame André for a whole year and knew the names of some of the streets. Also, Boitsfort was close to Brussels, which explained why she no longer spoke like the people of Marche.

There were just a few more questions to anticipate. Why had she been living in Boitsfort? Who was she living with? Where were her parents? The answers came to her in a flash. Her father had been taken away by the Germans as a prisoner of war. Régine had heard the term *prisonnier de guerre* and knew that it applied to soldiers. She could pretend that her father was a soldier. As for her mother, she could say that she too had been taken away, although this would be harder to explain because only men were really taken prisoners of war. Régine would have to think of something else to explain the absence of her mother and why her grandmother in Boitsfort was now taking care of her. But this wouldn't be too difficult. If anyone asked, Régine could even provide an address in Boitsfort.

She remembered the game she had played on the parquet floor in the house of Madame André. Now, in the darkness of Marie's bedroom, she invented a new game. This one had nothing to do with jumping squares. To win the game, she had to convince other people that she really was Augusta Dubois. And if I win, Régine told herself, Papa will come back.

Chapter Twenty-four

BUT NO ONE in the Carpentier house seemed to believe the story about her grandmother in Boitsfort, least of all Jean. He came to his own conclusion about Régine's odd behavior. In his mind, there was only one reason why she would act so mysteriously.

"You have big crooked fingers," he told Régine at breakfast one day. "Big fingers like dirty Jews."

Régine looked at her fingers. Were they dirty? Was she dirty? Were Jews dirty?

She was scratching her head more and more. Even when she didn't, she wanted to. She still couldn't comb out the tangled mess, and scratching was like combing.

Monsieur and Madame Carpentier also made their suspicions known, although they did so in a more subtle way.

"Our daughter Marie talks too much," Madame Carpentier told Régine. "You don't talk enough. Why is that?"

Régine did not dare talk. It was safer to say nothing. She had no idea what these people would do if they could prove she was Jewish. They might go to the Germans. So she simply ignored their comments and continued to play stupid. When confronted with questions, she stared at the floor and tried not to scratch her head.

Who would have known it could be so exhausting playing dumb?

One day, the postman brought a parcel addressed to

Augusta Dubois. It was wrapped in plain-brown paper and bore no return address. When Madame Carpentier gave her the parcel, Régine could feel from its edges that it was a book. She was so excited that she opened it right there at the front door.

The entire family looked on as she pulled the wrapping off the book. With enormous pleasure, she read the title to herself: *La case de l'Oncle Tom*. It was the French translation of *Uncle Tom's Cabin*. Just then a piece of paper fell from between the pages. Régine bent quickly to pick it up. She slipped the paper back into the book without even looking at it, and hoped that the others would think nothing of it.

"What was that?" asked Jean. Ever since that first day, he watched every move she made.

"Nothing," Régine said.

"It looked like a piece of paper."

"It's just a bookmark," she said.

She ran up the stairs to her room. She shut the door behind her and jumped on her bed. She opened the book to the page that held the piece of paper. It was a note containing only a few words. *"Je ne t'oublie pas"* — I have not forgotten you.

It was signed "Nicole."

Régine reached under the bed and grabbed her duffel bag. She slipped the note into the envelope, and put the envelope inside the book. She then put the book in the bag and pushed it under the bed for safekeeping.

"You're lucky," Marie said that night in the darkness of the room.

"Lucky? Why?"

"Because you got a present. Who sent it to you?" she asked. "Your parents?"

"No," Régine said.

"Who then?"

"A friend."

"How come your parents don't send you presents?"

"I'll get a present when my father gets back. He's a prisoner of war," Régine said.

Régine wondered whether she should speak to Marie about her family. It would be easy to tell her the truth in the dark, she thought. Marie was nice, not like her brother. She never made comments about "big crooked fingers" and "dirty Jews" like he often did. Unlike her parents, she never even hinted at such things. Marie was the only person in the family that Régine liked. But could she trust her?

Régine was glad she was able to start school the week after her arrival. She left the house early with Marie and walked along the dirt road that led past neighboring farms and into the village where the school was located.

The school was nothing like the big, stone building where she had gone to school in Brussels. It had only one classroom, filled with girls and boys of different ages. Régine was two years older than Marie but she still sat in the same classroom. She did not mind.

After class, Régine liked to do homework with Marie. Jean did not bother her then. She especially enjoyed French composition and grammar, always her best subjects. Here, too, the teacher seemed pleased with her work — just like Mademoiselle Descotte in Brussels. She wished her former teacher could see her now, tutoring Marie.

"Do you have any brothers or sisters?" Marie asked one night, when the light was off and both of them were in bed.

Régine thought about Léon and the men in army uniforms with their clubs and bayonets at la Gare du Midi. Then she wondered: Was Augusta supposed to have brothers? What about sisters?

"Go to sleep," she told Marie. "It's very late."

Chapter Twenty-five

A S THE DAYS PASSED, Régine began to feel more uncomfortable in school. Partly because of her accent, she was considered an outsider by the other children. Her avoidance of answering their questions also alienated them. One question would always lead to another. Better not answer the first.

One day on her way back from school she was confronted by a gang of boys in a field which she and Marie had to cross. The boys chased Régine across the field and, after catching up to her, tried to pull off her clothes. Régine was terrified and began to scream. She bit and kicked and managed to run free, dragging Marie after her. When she got back to the farm Marie told the story to her parents, who seemed to think that the episode was all Régine's doing.

Even in the schoolroom, things were not going as well as they should. Back in Brussels, Régine had sat at the front of the class because she did not want to miss anything and she had liked to be called upon to answer questions. Augusta Dubois sat in the last row and never raised her hand.

She soon had another reason for wanting to be at the back of the room. When she scratched her messy hair, a few small insects came out under her nails. She would try to drop them on the floor and crush them without any of the other students noticing she had lice.

She was so careful that even Madame Carpentier didn't

notice. But Madame Carpentier did see something else. One morning at breakfast, she stopped as she was about to remove a dish from the table.

"What's that on your hand?" she said, and grabbed Régine's hand to examine it. "There are scabs all over it. Let me see your other hand. And your legs. Pull down your stockings."

Régine stood up. The horror on Madame Carpentier's face deepened as she found scabs everywhere on Régine. "You've got *la gale!*" she screamed — scabies.

Madame Carpentier was like a crazy woman as she went to work to get rid of the parasitic mites under Régine's skin. She was terrified they would infest the rest of the family. She told Marie to stay away as she carried basins into the bedroom. It was while she was scrubbing Régine and rubbing her with a sticky yellow lotion which stank of ammonia that she found the lice in Régine's hair.

Madame Carpentier knew what to do about that, too. She took her scissors and cut off Régine's hair as close to the scalp as she could, then poured vinegar over her head and plunged it into a strong stinging liquid.

Twice a day for the next several days, Régine went through the scrubbing, the smearing and the dousing. Embarrassed as she was by it all, she felt a certain relief that something was being done to get rid of the itching.

Her next worry was returning to school. Everyone would guess why her hair was cut off.

She need not have worried. Three days later, Madame Carpentier told her to pack her bag. Only a month and a half had passed but the Carpentiers had had enough of Augusta Dubois. They were sending her away.

Chapter Twenty-six

RÉGINE PULLED her canvas bag from under the bed and began to fill it. It was a morning in late November, her last day in Andoumont. There was a knock on the door and Marie entered the room. She sat on the edge of the bed. "Mama says you're going to your grandmother's in Boitsfort. Is that true?" she asked.

"My grandmother's?" Régine said, holding a sweater against her chest. She had not figured out her next step, but she certainly didn't want to return to Madame André.

"Yes, I heard her on the telephone. She spoke to the people who brought you here."

"I can't go to my grandmother's," Régine said.

"Why not?"

Because I don't have a grandmother in Boitsfort, Régine thought, but said: "Oh, she's very old. I can't go back there."

"Mama says you can't stay here anymore. I heard her on the telephone. They're sending someone over right away."

"Now?"

"That's what Mama says. A man from *Aide paysanne* is coming to get you."

Marie went downstairs and Régine resumed packing. At a time like this, it was important to think very clearly.

The first problem was lying about having a grandmother in Boitsfort. How could she explain this grandmother did not exist? Admitting that she had lied would draw further suspicion. Questions would be asked. Anything might happen if the man from *Aide paysanne* found out she was Jewish. He might tell on her, or tell someone else who might tell the Germans.

She had two options. The first was to pretend that Madame André really was her grandmother. She could tell the man from *Aide paysanne* to take her to the house in Boitsfort. But she could not warn Madame André beforehand and did not know how the old woman would react. She might deny the whole story and tell the truth about Régine Miller.

No, Régine thought. Better to stay away from Madame André altogether.

Her second option was to say nothing at all. If the man asked about her grandmother, Régine would just stare at the floor and not say a word. He could not take her to Madame André's house if she did not tell him where she lived.

Yes, Régine decided. That was the best thing to do.

Then came the other problem. Where would he take her? Who would look after her from now on? Régine could think of only one person who could help her, and that was Nicole. But Régine had not heard a word from her, except for the book that had arrived in the mail without a return address. Nicole had to be very careful, Régine thought, as she packed the book with the rest of her belongings into her duffel bag.

Her thoughts were interrupted by a knock at the door. Marie poked her head inside the bedroom. "Mama says to come down now," she said. "The man from *Aide paysanne* is here."

Régine carried her bag downstairs where Madame Carpentier was standing with the man near the door. Madame Carpentier handed Régine her ration book. The man had kept his winter coat on and seemed anxious to leave right away. Monsieur Carpentier and his son Jean were nowhere to be seen. Régine was not surprised they had not come to say good-bye.

The man stepped forward and said, "I'm going to take you home. To Boitsfort."

He knew where she had lived before coming here.

There was nothing she could do.

Chapter Twenty-seven

A T THE VILLAGE TERMINAL they caught the bus back to
Brussels. Neither of them spoke during the entire ride.
The man seemed anxious for it to end, and was constantly
looking out the window and then at his watch. Régine was
too afraid to speak. What would happen when they got to
Madame André's?

She had visions of the man calling her Augusta in front
of the old woman.

"But no, Monsieur," Madame André would say. "Her
name is Régine Miller. She is not my granddaughter. She is
from Brussels."

What would happen if the man discovered she was Jewish? Would he tell the Germans? Régine shuddered at the
thought of what would happen next. She closed her eyes and
saw the German soldiers running toward her, surrounding her,
shouting at her, taking her away.

The bus pulled into the city terminal. Somehow the trip
back had seemed much shorter than the ride out to the
countryside. From the station, they took the trams to
Boitsfort, got off and made their way to Madame André's
house. Régine's fear grew as they approached the familiar
house. The drapes were drawn at the front window, the same
window where she had spent so many hours waiting for her
father to take her home.

The man pushed open the gate, walked to the front door and knocked loudly.

Régine heard the sound of footsteps beyond the door, and then the familiar voice of Madame André.

"Who's there?"

"*Aide paysanne!*" the man called out.

"Who?"

"*Aide paysanne!*" he said. "I have Augusta with me!"

"Who?" said Madame André.

The man shook his head. "Is she deaf?"

"She's very old," Régine said nervously.

"Open the door!" he called out.

Don't open the door, Régine said to herself. Please don't open the door.

She did not know how it would help her, but she did not want the door to open. She did not want Madame André to speak to the man and risk giving away her secret. She would rather wait outside all day if she had to.

"Who's there?" Madame André asked again.

"*Aide paysanne,*" repeated the man. "Augusta is here."

"You have the wrong house," Madame André said.

The man threw up his hands.

"She's very old," Régine repeated.

The man tried again and the door opened.

Madame André stood staring at Régine. "*C'est toi? Qu'est-ce que tu fais ici?*" — It's you? What are you doing here?

Régine watched with relief as the man turned and walked out the gate. As far as he was concerned, he had taken Augusta Dubois to her grandmother's house. His job was done. He had no intention of spending the rest of the day arguing with a deaf old woman.

"I have nowhere else to go," Régine said quietly to Madame André.

"Well, you're not staying here! I'm going to call someone right away! You shouldn't have come!"

Madame André grabbed Régine by the elbow and dragged her into the house. She shut the door and marched into the kitchen. Régine followed behind, rubbing her elbow.

Madame André opened a drawer, rummaged through it and pulled out a slip of paper. She picked up the phone and dialed. "I have a message for Nicole," she said.

Régine sat down, relieved to hear that name again.

"Yes, right away," Madame André said into the phone. "I want her out of my house."

She put down the receiver and turned to Régine: "It's done. They're coming to get you. Go wait in the other room. I've got work to do." Then, as an afterthought, she added: "What happened to your hair?"

"They cut it off," Régine answered, embarrassed.

Madame André did not ask why. Perhaps she knew. Or she didn't care.

Régine carried her bag out of the kitchen. She went into the study and sat in the chair in front of the window. She looked over at the house next door and saw that it was dark. Where was Madame Charles? Had she gone away somewhere? She wanted to ask Madame André but did not want to cause any more trouble. She sat quietly for hours it seemed and looked out at the empty road. Memories of all the hours she had waited at the window flooded back. When at last she saw a lone figure approaching from far away, she imagined a man in a gray overcoat and fedora coming to the gate. Now he was pushing it open...

She jumped awake at the sound of the knock on the door.

"Hold on," Madame André said, emerging from the kitchen. "Go sit down. I'll get it."

But Régine did not sit down. She stood behind Madame

André as the old woman opened the door. She was too excited about seeing Nicole again. The door opened. It was not Nicole.

The visitor was a man Régine had never seen before.

"I've come for the girl," he said.

The man spoke quickly as if he did not want to waste time. He did not say "Bonjour," announce who he was or where he was from. Madame André did not speak either. She motioned to Régine to get her bag and go.

Chapter Twenty-eight

THEY WENT BACK to the bus station in Brussels before the man finally spoke to her.

"You are going back to Liège," he said. "Another family has been found for you. In Lagrange."

On the bus, he told her a little more. "You will stay with Monsieur and Madame Wathieu. They live on a farm and have no children. They look forward to having an extra hand around the house."

Régine wanted to ask about Nicole but thought better of it. She did not know who this man was, whether he was from *Aide paysanne* or the Jewish resistance.

Would this new family be any nicer than the last two? Why had Nicole not come to get her? Had something happened to her?

It was a bitterly cold night as they got off the bus in Lagrange. The man took a paper out of his pocket and studied the directions. As they walked toward the home of Monsieur and Madame Wathieu, Régine buried one hand in the pocket of her coat to keep it warm, while she carried her duffel bag with the other. She could see a few small lights in the darkness. All was silent except for the crunch of snow under their feet.

At last they arrived at what looked like a very large farmhouse and went up the path. Before the man had a chance to knock, the door swung open. A man, a woman and a small black dog stood there as if they had been waiting and watching.

Madame Wathieu greeted them with a smile. "Come in. It's cold," she said. "There's a fire in the kitchen to help you warm up. Are you hungry? You must be tired."

The man shook his head. "I must be going. I have to take the bus back tonight."

"Are you sure?" asked Monsieur Wathieu. "We can offer you something to eat."

"There's no time," said the man, adding: "This is Augusta, the little girl you will be looking after."

Régine gave a nod and said, "Good evening, madame."

Madame Wathieu smiled and bent down to look into Régine's face. "Hello, Augusta. Welcome. We're happy you're here."

Monsieur Wathieu held out his hand. "Hello, Augusta," he said. "How are you?"

"I'm well, thank you, monsieur," Régine answered.

"The bus ride wasn't too long, I hope?"

"No, monsieur."

"Cold out there, isn't it?"

"Yes, monsieur."

"There's a fire in the kitchen. Why don't you take your coat off and go warm up?"

"Thank you, monsieur."

"But there's just one thing you must stop doing. You must stop calling me monsieur. My name is Pierre."

His wife laughed. "And I'm Sylvie. No more monsieur and madame. We're going to be friends for the next three months. Agreed?"

"Yes," Régine said shyly.

The man gave some last-minute instructions. "Give Monsieur and Madame Wathieu your ration book," he said to Régine. Then he spoke to Madame Wathieu. "If you have any questions or problems," he said, "here is the number to call."

"What can possibly go wrong?" Sylvie Wathieu asked.

Régine repeated the words to herself as she entered the kitchen. *What can possibly go wrong?* Everywhere things had gone wrong. Would it be different here? She had a good feeling about the Wathieus. It was the first time since leaving home — a year and a half ago — that she had not been made to feel like an intruder. She hoped they could be friends. But part of her was terribly afraid of being disappointed once again.

In the kitchen, Régine had a chance to observe them. They were older than her parents but not as old as Madame André. Pierre wore a jacket over his shirt and trousers, and wooden clogs on his feet. Sylvie wore a dark-colored dress which almost touched the ground and had an apron tied over it. She also wore wooden clogs.

The kitchen was large and warmed by a big, wood-burning stove. The dog lay down beside it. A spinning wheel stood on one side of the room and an old radio on the other. It had the same big knobs and short legs as the one her parents owned.

Régine walked over to the dog and bent down to pet him. He looked very old. He gazed up at her with tired eyes as she scratched behind his ears, then, satisfied with her, he closed his eyes and went back to sleep. He looked like a cross between a French poodle and a sheepdog.

This was her first contact with a dog since she was very little. Before moving to 73 rue Van Lint, the Millers had lived in another apartment in Brussels, and kept a small dog named Diane. One day the dog bit Régine on the lip. Her father promptly got rid of the dog, despite Régine's cries and pleas to bring her back. The scar never disappeared.

Chapter Twenty-Nine

REMEMBERING DIANE brought memories of that first apartment. It was on boulevard de la Révision and many Jewish families from Poland lived in the building. They used to come to Régine's mother for all kinds of help. This was how it was back then, before her mother fell ill. Régine remembered herself as a tiny girl, falling asleep with her mother bending over her and singing the same cradle songs in Yiddish her grandmother had sung to her when she was little. Sometimes Mrs. Miller told wonderful stories about life in Poland, about her parents and brothers and sisters, especially about her youngest brother, Shlomo, who had been her favorite, the same Oncle Shlomo who was now living in England. Was he alive? Did he know, Régine wondered, what had happened to her mother?

Two tiny kittens scurried out of the kitchen. Régine was shaken out of her sad thoughts. The mother cat came along next, at a more leisurely pace, and Régine sat down on the floor to pet it with her left hand, while her right hand went on petting the dog. It was good to sit in the warmth of the stove.

"His name is Marquis," said Pierre Wathieu from the doorway.

"He likes to be petted," Régine said.

Pierre laughed. "He's getting old. He has ulcers, but he still works hard. Without Marquis, I wouldn't be able to run this farm."

"What does he do?"

"He helps me round up the cows."

"Round them up?"

"For milking. When they're out in the pasture he helps me bring them into the barn. Have you ever milked a cow, Augusta?"

"I don't know how," Régine said.

"I'll show you."

"I'll be glad to help," Régine said shyly, "if you show me what to do."

"Would you like something to eat?" Sylvie Wathieu interrupted. "You must be hungry."

Régine shook her head. "No, thank you." She was hungry but was too shy to say so.

"I'll show you how to milk a cow tomorrow," Pierre said. "But school comes first. We'll go to the village to get you enrolled."

"I like school," Régine said. "One day I want to be a teacher."

"Good." He turned and looked up at a clock on the wall. "You should be going to bed. Look at the time."

Régine looked up and saw that it was 10 p.m. That was not all she noticed. Something else hung on the wall directly above the clock. She had missed it when she first entered the kitchen, but now that she'd seen it she couldn't take her eyes off it. She knew it meant the people were Catholic. It was a cross, but Régine had never seen one in a house before. There had been none on the walls of the other houses she had stayed in.

"Your room is ready," Madame Wathieu said. "Come along upstairs."

Régine went to the front door to pick up her duffel bag. There she saw another cross hanging above the door.

On the landing at the top of the stairs she passed a semicircular dish made of brass screwed into the wall. The dish was filled with water. Régine wondered what it was meant for. She followed Madame Wathieu into a little bedroom straight ahead. Above the door hung another cross. Every door in the hallway had a cross.

As she watched Madame Wathieu throw an extra blanket over the bed, she realized she would have a room to herself for the first time since leaving Madame André's. Over the big, comfortable-looking bed hung another cross. The Wathieus must be very religious, she decided.

"You'll need the extra blanket because it's going to be a cold, cold night," Madame Wathieu said.

"Thank you, madame."

"Don't say madame. Say, 'Sylvie.' "

"Thank you," Régine paused and then added, "Sylvie."

Sylvie was about to go when she asked quietly, "What happened to your hair?"

"It was cut off," Régine said, embarrassed.

Sylvie seemed about to ask another question, but changed her mind. "It'll grow back. They say it grows back prettier than before." She paused at the door. "If you need anything during the night, please don't be shy."

"Thank you," Régine said.

"Good night," said Sylvie Wathieu. She left, pulling the door shut behind her.

Régine dropped her bag on the bed and looked around. The walls were bare except for the cross above the bed and, on the opposite wall, a framed picture of a mother and child with halos around their heads. There was a window, a dresser with a pitcher of water and a washbowl on it and a mirror above it. A night table beside the bed held a small lamp that provided the only light in the room.

104

Régine walked over to the window, and pressed her face against the glass. Outside, she saw nothing but darkness. She walked back to the bed and began to unpack, slowly transferring her folded clothes to the dresser, one item at a time. After she finished, she pulled out *Uncle Tom's Cabin* from the bag and placed it on the night table.

All that traveling had made her very tired. In the darkness she sensed the eyes of the figure on the cross above her head looking down on her and the mother and child staring out of the picture across the room. She was exhausted and yet, for some reason, she could not fall asleep.

Chapter Thirty

RÉGINE FELT she had been awake all night when the morning sunlight streamed into the room. She pushed back the covers and hopped off the high bed to look out the window. Her room overlooked the backyard of the farmhouse and a bare winter orchard. A few pigs were rubbing themselves against the tree trunks, as if trying to generate some warmth. Beyond the orchard were woods.

She got dressed, made her bed and headed for the stairs, noticing again the dish full of water. She went downstairs to the kitchen.

"Good morning, Augusta," Pierre said. "Did you sleep well?"

"Yes," Régine lied.

"Good. You'll be ready to join me for work on the farm, then," he chuckled.

"Pierre, school comes first. We must enroll her," his wife said.

"Tomorrow is time enough," he said. "Today she can get used to the place."

Sylvie placed some fresh-baked bread on the table, along with butter, jam and cottage cheese. A pot of coffee was brewing on the stove.

"There can't be too many farms in the town of Marche," Pierre went on.

Sylvie brought the coffee pot to the table.

"Have you lived in Marche all your life?" she asked.

"No," Régine said nervously.

"How long did you live there?"

Régine reached for a piece of bread, stalling for time. She thought about the story she had told before. Would these people believe it?

"I haven't lived in Marche for a long time," she said. "I live with my grandmother in Boitsfort now."

"Boitsfort?" Sylvie asked. "Where's that?"

"Near Brussels," Régine said.

"Brussels!" Pierre said. "We really do have a city girl on our hands!"

Sylvie did not seem to share her husband's amusement. Something else was on her mind, and she gave Régine a puzzled look.

"Where are your parents?" she asked.

"My parents?" Régine kept her eyes on her piece of bread, which she held in her hand. "Papa's a prisoner of war."

"A prisoner of war," Pierre said, suddenly showing concern. "He must have been a very brave soldier, your father."

"Yes, he is," said Régine.

"What about your mother?" Sylvie asked.

Régine did not have a story to explain her mother's absence. She kept her eyes fixed on the piece of bread as she blurted out: "I don't know."

The room fell silent and Régine sensed right away that she had said the wrong thing. She looked up and saw Pierre and Sylvie glance at each other. "You don't know?" Pierre asked. His voice was kind, but the question was asked.

"No," Régine said, lowering her eyes again.

"How can you not know?" Pierre looked at his wife.

Sylvie shook her head to cut him off, then Régine heard her whisper, "Walking the streets? You know Brussels."

107

The room became quiet again. The friendly atmosphere changed to one of tension. Pierre reached for some bread and jam and Sylvie did the same.

Régine could not eat. She did not know exactly what it meant to be "walking the streets" but she knew it was not nice. She was ashamed at not being able to respond to such an insult to her mother. Yet all she could do was say nothing and stare blankly, as she had learned to do in these uncomfortable situations.

Chapter Thirty-One

AFTER BREAKFAST, the three got dressed to go outside. Pierre wore a heavy coat and traded his wooden clogs for rubber boots. Sylvie did the same. She had an extra pair of boots for Régine. Régine pulled on the boots, then slipped into her coat and followed them out the door. Marquis was already running up ahead.

She gazed with pleasure around the front yard of the farm. The latrine was at the side of the main house. The Wathieus had no indoor plumbing. For washing, there was a big trough built to hold rainwater. Pierre explained how to carry water to the house in two buckets strung across the shoulders. At the bottom of the field there was a spring for drinking water.

They visited the barn and the pigsty, and finally the cowshed. All were dark and smelly. Régine counted seven cows, each in a separate stall under the low, wooden ceiling.

Pierre asked her to choose a cow.

Régine was startled. "What do you mean?"

"The cows," he said. "Pick any one. Pick your favorite."

Régine shrugged and pointed to the cow in the first stall.

"Okay," Pierre said. "From now on, that will be your cow. That means she's your responsibility. You'll milk her and keep her fed and clean. Do you think you can do it?"

"I — I don't know how," stammered Régine.

"I'll show you," Sylvie offered. She dragged a low stool into the stall.

"Don't you want to know her name?" Pierre asked.

"Her name?"

"All my cows have a name. Yours is called La Blanque."

La Blanque was Walloon for *la blanche*, meaning the white one. The name was appropriate. La Blanque was completely white.

Régine watched Sylvie sit on the low stool and reach under La Blanque to milk her. The first step, she was told, was always to wear a handkerchief on her head. The reason for this became clear as Sylvie went to work. La Blanque had the annoying habit of swinging her tail at the face of the person milking her.

Régine got her first lesson in how to milk a cow but her hands grew tired quickly and she had to stop. Sylvie did not seem to mind and she finished milking La Blanque. "Don't worry," she said. "You'll get used to it. It takes practice."

Régine then helped carry the full buckets out past the barn to the milk room which was attached to the farmhouse. She walked slowly in her big rubber boots, being careful not to spill any of the top cream. The milk room held a machine that Pierre said was used to separate the milk from the cream. Another machine turned the milk into butter and cheese. Régine emptied her buckets into one of the metal containers and went back to the cowshed for more.

After the milking was done, she helped sweep the cowshed with a heavy broom. Sylvie shoveled dung into a wheelbarrow which Pierre pushed to the manure heap out front. Régine did not mind the work. She even enjoyed it, because Pierre and Sylvie worked hard, too.

In the afternoon, Régine went with Sylvie to the village to register for school while Pierre continued to work on the farm. The school was at the end of the village. When they arrived Régine saw that it was almost identical to the village school she had attended in Andoumont.

Inside they met the teacher, a man this time. Sylvie introduced Régine as Augusta Dubois and said she was visiting for three months.

"Does your class have room for one more girl?"

"Of course," the teacher said. The school had only one classroom and boys and girls studied together. "We always have room for another student." He pulled a book from his desk and wrote down Régine's name: Augusta Dubois.

On the way back to the farm Régine saw a building she had not noticed on their way to the school. It was up the road beyond the farm, a kind of fort. What caused her to stop was the sight of a German flag waving above it.

"Why is the German flag there?" she asked, suddenly frightened.

"German soldiers," Sylvie explained. "They've been stationed there since the occupation began."

"Do they stay there all the time?" asked Régine. She tried not to sound too concerned.

"What do you mean?" said Sylvie.

"I mean, do they ever come to the farm?"

"Yes, sometimes," Sylvie said. "They go to all the farms."

Régine was terrified. "What for?" *To look for Jewish children?*

"For food. They come whenever they want and take whatever they want."

Régine pictured the soldiers at the Gare du Midi with their clubs and bayonets. She looked up and saw that Sylvie sensed her fear.

"Don't worry. They won't hurt us. All they're interested in is food. And they need us to stay alive to provide it."

But Régine did not feel better as they resumed their walk back to the farm. Sylvie went on talking, trying to reassure her.

"They'd be foolish to hurt us," she was saying. "They need us for bread, eggs, butter, milk. Sometimes they take a whole pig or a cow. They have nothing against us. They give us forms to fill out so that they can keep track of everything — so complicated, these German forms! Most of the old farmers around here can't even read them! They have to come and ask Pierre."

As she walked beside Sylvie, Régine stared at the fort in the distance. It was true that the German soldiers had no reason to hurt her, as long as they did not discover she was Jewish. *Tell no one who you are*, Régine said to herself and pressed her fingers tightly into her palms. *Not even Pierre and Sylvie*.

Chapter Thirty-two

THAT NIGHT, after supper, Pierre lit a pipe and sat down next to the stove to read the newspaper while Régine and Sylvie washed the dishes and put them away. Bricks had been placed in the stove and would later be wrapped up in cloth to be used upstairs as bed warmers. After he finished with the paper, Pierre leaned over and turned on the radio.

Soon there was a knock at the door and Régine felt her heart stop with fear. She was relieved to see the knock announced some of the old farmers Sylvie had mentioned. *"Ils viennent pour la soirée"* — they're coming for the evening, she told Régine. It was their nightly routine to gather and read the newspaper and listen to the radio. Two of them came in together, pulled up chairs and sat with Pierre in front of the stove, while Marquis continued his snoozing at their feet. Within minutes a third man — "Old Mr. Bertrand," Sylvie whispered — arrived and joined the others.

Pierre introduced the three old men to Augusta Dubois: "The girl I told you about. She will be staying for three months." This sparked a lot of interest from the visitors.

It frightened Régine to think that the Wathieus seemed to have informed everyone in Lagrange about her arrival. The less people knew about her the better. She hoped she wouldn't be asked questions about her family. She nodded to the three men.

They were talking in Walloon among themselves. She was

beginning to pick it up after having spent a month and a half in Wallonie with the Carpentier family in Andoumont.

Monsieur Bertrand turned to her suddenly and, speaking French, suggested that she visit his farm to meet his granddaughter, Irene.

"The two of you could be friends," he said. "We live in the last house in the village."

"I will try to come," Régine said quietly.

"Irene is seventeen," said Monsieur Bertrand. "How old are you?"

"Eleven," said Régine.

"Eleven!" the man said with surprise. "You look much older than eleven."

Régine did not respond. She had never thought of herself as looking older than her age. She tried to remember Augusta Dubois's birthdate. Was it on the ration book she had given the Wathieus? She must be more careful.

The old men soon lost interest in Régine and began to discuss recent reports of the war on the radio and in the newspaper, *La Libre Belgique*.

The war had turned in favor of the Allies. The Germans had been defeated in Russia and were now suffering heavy losses in the Allied campaign to liberate Italy. The old men were hopeful that the war would end soon, so that their sons and grandsons would return home. While the men talked Régine helped Sylvie peel potatoes for the next day while the cats hung around waiting for her to throw them a piece of raw potato. Now and then Sylvie would doze off, then wake with a start and continue peeling. As Régine listened to the men talking of the war's end, she made up her mind: her father would definitely return with the others after the victory.

Finally, when the potatoes were peeled, Régine said good night and went upstairs to prepare for bed. She was beginning to feel better. Her first day with Pierre and Sylvie had passed without any difficulties. It was a good start, much better than with the other three families.

In her bedroom, Régine washed with rainwater using the pitcher and bowl and then changed into her night clothes. It was cold in the room. She realized that she had forgotten to bring up one of the bricks that had been warming in the oven downstairs. She opened the door of her room and was on her way down the stairs just as Pierre and Sylvie were coming up. The visitors had left and the Wathieus were on their way to bed.

They met at the top of the stairs right next to the dish of water.

"Where are you going?" Pierre asked.

"Downstairs, to get a brick from the oven," Régine said.

"Don't bother," said Pierre. "I have them right here." He held out a brick wrapped in cloth.

"Thank you," she said.

Then the two of them did something unexpected. As Régine looked on, Sylvie reached over, dipped her fingers into the dish of water, and touched her forehead and shoulders. Then Pierre did the same. Régine now knew why the dish of water was there. She had often seen Belgians cross themselves, but this was the first time she had seen it done in someone's house with actual water.

She turned to go to her room, but Sylvie's voice stopped her.

"Augusta, haven't you forgotten something?"

Régine turned to face her. "Pardon?"

"The holy water," Sylvie said, nodding at the dish.

"Oh," Régine said.

She looked at Pierre and Sylvie and realized she was supposed to do as they had done. She tried to copy them as best she could but must have done it badly because of the way they looked at her.

She was glad to escape back to her bedroom. She lay on the bed looking at the picture of the mother and child with the halo on the wall and then at the cross on the wall above her head. "I must be more careful and watch everything they do," she told herself.

The next day Sylvie asked Régine if she had a rosary. Régine did not know what a rosary was. When she shook her head, Sylvie went to a drawer and gave her a string of beads. "Do you know how to use it?" Sylvie asked. She did not seem surprised when Régine said no.

Sylvie took out her own rosary and led Régine through prayers: *Notre père qui êtes aux cieux* and *Sainte Marie, mère de Dieu*.

Later that day in the kitchen, Sylvie said: "We're going to communion tomorrow. Would you like to come with us?" Régine looked uncertain. Sylvie stared at her suspiciously, then asked: "Augusta, have you been baptized?"

"Of course she's been baptized!" Pierre said angrily.

"Shhh!" said Sylvie. "Let her answer. Don't be afraid, Augusta. You can tell us."

Régine stared at the floor. *Tell no one who you are.*

"Have you been baptized or not?"

"I don't know."

She raised her eyes and again saw that this was a mistake. Pierre and Sylvie were only more puzzled.

"How can you not know?"

"I don't remember."

"Didn't your parents tell you?"

Régine didn't answer.

"We'll talk to Monsieur Le Vicaire," Sylvie said. "He'll know what to do."

Régine swallowed. She knew classmates in Brussels who were Catholic. She knew that they had their first communion all dressed in pretty white dresses and that Jewish girls did not. She knew also that confirmation was not just for one day. It was forever.

"Maybe she is baptized," Pierre said.

"What do you mean?" Sylvie asked.

"Augusta doesn't know whether or not her parents baptized her," he said. "What if they did?"

Sylvie shrugged. "Better twice than never."

She turned to Régine.

"Don't worry, Augusta. We'll talk to Monsieur Le Vicaire tomorrow when we go to church."

What should she do if Monsieur Le Vicaire wanted to baptize her? What would her father want her to do? When he returned, what would he say?

Chapter Thirty-three

THE NEXT MORNING, Sunday, life changed on the Wathieu farm. No work would be done on the farm that day, except for the essential tasks of feeding and milking the cows, and tending to the chickens and pigs. As soon as the animals were looked after, Pierre and Sylvie changed into what they called their "Sunday clothes." Sylvie put on a dark dress and a small black hat, and Pierre, a dark suit with a gold chain that ran across the vest.

Pierre and Sylvie were waiting by the front door when Régine came down wearing her best dress. They put on overcoats and set out on the forty-minute walk along the dirt road that led to the church beyond the village.

Along the way Pierre and Sylvie discussed how they would meet Monsieur Le Vicaire after the service to ask about a baptism for Régine. Régine kept her hands in the pockets of her coat and walked in silence.

The church was a small, stone building with a steeple. People were arriving from every direction. Most were old and dressed in dark-colored clothes. Some of the men wore caps, which they removed as they walked through the door.

Pierre let Régine and Sylvie go in ahead of him. From the back, Régine saw that almost all the pews were full. Monsieur Le Vicaire was standing at the altar in front. He had already begun the service, and his voice echoed, bouncing off the ceiling.

Régine was about to walk up the aisle when she felt a tap on the shoulder. She turned and saw Sylvie nodding at a dish of holy water on the wall. It was made of brass in the shape of a semicircle, just like the one at the farmhouse. Régine dipped her fingers in the holy water, made the sign of the cross and hoped no one was looking to see if she did it correctly.

They walked up the aisle and found a place near the front. Régine moved into the pew first. Only then did she notice that Sylvie and Pierre had gone down on one knee in the middle of the aisle and, facing the altar, made the sign of the cross. Then they took their seats next to Régine. *Be more careful*, she warned herself.

For the next hour, Régine learned how to behave by watching the people around her. She knelt when they knelt. When they sat, she sat. When they stood up, she got up. When they prayed, she mumbled something to herself. She felt the eyes of Pierre and Sylvie watching her from either side, and she tried not to let it show that she was copying.

But her motions were always one step behind those of everyone else. Pierre and Sylvie would have no more doubt. It would be clear to them that the parents of Augusta Dubois had not raised their daughter to be "a good Catholic."

When they went to take communion, Pierre and Sylvie told her to wait in the pew while they went up with others to kneel before the altar. Régine watched as Monsieur Le Vicaire placed the wafer on their tongues. Were you supposed to bite on it or swallow it whole, Régine wondered. What did it taste like?

After the service, Régine waited outside the church while Pierre and Sylvie went to the rectory to speak with Monsieur Le Vicaire. The smiles on their faces when they came out told Régine everything before they even spoke. Yes, they said, it was settled. The vicar would arrange for the baptism of Augusta Dubois.

That night Régine lay awake, thinking of how she might talk her way out of the baptism. In the end, she drew a blank. There seemed to be no way out. Pierre and Sylvie were now convinced that Augusta Dubois had not been baptized. At least they still believed that she was Augusta Dubois from Marche and that was more important than anything else. She had played her part so well, it had never entered their minds that she might be Jewish. In their world, everyone was Catholic.

Even in the darkness, she felt she could see the mother and child on the wall — "*La Vierge Marie et le petit enfant Jésus,*" as Sylvie called them. Pierre and Sylvie were the most religious people she had ever met. The only other person who came close was her mother, but that was different. Her mother was religious in a different way.

She kept a kosher kitchen, prepared meals according to proper ritual, and stored special dishes in a glass cabinet for Passover. And like all observant Jewish housewives, she kept two sets of dishes for everyday use: one for dairy and the other for meat.

Régine remembered the photograph of her grandfather, her father's father, who was still living in Poland when the Germans invaded. The photograph showed a distinguished-looking man dressed in black and wearing a long, white beard in the Jewish religious tradition. He looked nothing like her father, who was clean-shaven, modern-looking and not at all religious.

Régine's father did not go to the synagogue or observe Jewish holidays. He told Régine that he did not believe in God. When Régine looked at the photo of her grandfather in

Poland, she wondered how her father could have gotten along with him. Father and son seemed just so different. As she grew up, she came to believe her father had come to Belgium to escape the religious tradition of his family.

Sometimes Régine's mother scolded her father for saying there was no God. "Is this what you're teaching our children?" her mother would say. "That their religion has no importance?"

"It's more important they care about people," her father insisted.

On Saturdays, her mother put on her best clothes and walked alone to the synagogue, an old, dilapidated building in the rear of Régine's school. Twice a year, on Rosh Hashanah and Yom Kippur, Régine and Léon accompanied her to synagogue. Her father never went. As Léon got older, he joined the men and Régine sat with her mother and the other women as the rabbi performed the service.

Lying alone in her bed, Régine could almost hear her parents arguing. How could her father be so sure that God did not exist? And how could her mother be equally sure that He did? Which of them was right, and which was wrong?

What to make of it all? Her mother believed in God but her father didn't. Pierre and Sylvie believed in a different God, three Gods in one. Was there really a God, any God, somewhere, looking after people? If so, why didn't He stop the war and bring back her parents and brother?

Régine was finally getting sleepy. She closed her eyes and invented a new game to play in the darkness of her room.

"If Papa comes back," she said to herself, "then I will believe in God."

It was more a bet than a game. Or maybe it was like bargaining. There were no real rules, and there was nothing she had to do, such as crossing the room without stepping on

121

a crack. To win this game, all she had to do was wait. When she thought about it, maybe it was a bit like praying.

In the meantime, how could she postpone the baptism? She would say she wanted to wait for spring, that the war might be over and her father would come back. In any case, her three months at the Wathieus' would be over before then.

Chapter Thirty-four

RÉGINE HAD LOOKED FORWARD to going to school but she knew from the first day she attended that it was not going to work. All the subjects that the teacher covered, Régine had learned from Mademoiselle Descotte back at the *école primaire* in Brussels. Régine was far too advanced for the village school even though she was not one of the older students. The teacher realized this, too. After the first two weeks, as the other students worked on spelling and arithmetic, Régine was granted a special exemption from the regular curriculum and given a desk by herself at the back of the class where she spent her days dipping a nib in ink and practicing calligraphy.

The following week the teacher sent her home, explaining to Pierre and Sylvie that his one-classroom school had nothing to offer a bright student like Augusta Dubois. Pierre and Sylvie thanked the teacher and gave Régine the kind of smile that proud parents give their children.

Life at the farm settled into a routine that was some comfort to Régine while she waited for the war to end. She had the feeling everyone — the Wathieus, the old men who came in the evenings, the people in church — was also waiting for what they called "*la libération.*" For Régine the liberation meant the return of her father. Maybe Léon too. He was young and strong. Maybe Monsieur Gaspar was wrong about him. But her mother? She had been so sick: the pale face in the hospital bed, the frail hand held out, almost pleading. Could she really believe her mother had come through two more years of trouble? She would not think of her mother. Just her father and brother.

Every Sunday was the same. Going to church was only part of the day's ritual that started early in the morning and ended late at night. As time passed, she knew it by heart.

After the morning service she returned with Pierre and Sylvie to the farmhouse for lunch, which Sylvie prepared in the morning and left to simmer on the stove while they were away.

Sunday dinner was the most important meal of the week. It was the only meal for which a chicken was killed. Pierre, it turned out, was far too squeamish for such things, so it was always Sylvie who went into the barn. Sometimes Régine went with her. She was convinced the chickens knew what was coming the minute Sylvie came through the door. It was an eerie feeling, being watched by all those knowing birds. Sylvie seemed aware of this, too, and tried to act nonchalant. She would take the chicken outside before strangling it, but Régine was certain the other chickens sensed what was happening. Later, she always had a hard time swallowing her Sunday dinner.

After dinner, the three of them walked back to the church for afternoon services.

Later in the afternoon, they would sit in the living room, still dressed in their Sunday clothes. Pierre would read the *Évangile* while Sylvie and Régine brought out their rosaries. Together they recited the prayers — both prayers for each bead — until suppertime.

After supper, they read and prayed some more until bedtime. The Wathieus permitted Régine to read the two or three books they had in the house, which all had something to do with Jesus. No other reading was allowed. Régine put away *Uncle Tom's Cabin* after Pierre and Sylvie saw it and deemed it was "not fit for a Catholic household." That left nothing but stories about children loving Baby Jesus, which she read and reread. In retrospect, her stay with Madame André in Boitsfort seemed less bleak. The old woman might have been cold and indifferent, but she did have a wonderful room full of books. Even better, Régine thought, she did not have to pretend she was someone else.

Sylvie also gave her a blue-enamel medal of the Virgin Mary — Notre Dame de Lourdes — along with firm instructions to carry it with her at all times. Sylvie had been to the shroud of Bernadette in Lourdes in southwestern France many years before and brought back the medal as a good luck charm. Régine accepted it and kept it in her pocket. It might help bring luck to her father, and maybe even Léon, she thought.

By Christmas, Régine had not only learned the prayers but also the service at the village church. She no longer had to watch the others to know when to sit, stand or kneel and when to reply "amen" during the sermon by Monsieur Le Vicaire. On Christmas Eve they went to midnight mass. Régine thought it was beautiful. From her pew, she had a good view of the life-size manger in front of the altar with the figures huddled around the baby Jesus. It was a family. The animals were lovely, too. She sang hymns from her song book, along with the choir whose voices resounded in the church. At home she tried to go up to bed ahead of Sylvie and Pierre to avoid crossing herself with the holy water. But when either was nearby, she no longer needed to watch them to know what she had to do.

Chapter Thirty-five

FARM WORK took up the days of the week while everyone waited for the war to end. Italy had surrendered but everyone knew the war could not end until the Allies landed somewhere in France or Belgium and drove the Germans out. When would that be?

Régine helped both inside and outside the house. There was milking La Blanque, sweeping the barn, shoveling dung, finding the eggs the hens had laid. After that, there was feeding the chickens and bringing up water from the spring in two buckets strung across her shoulders. She was glad Pierre's special preserve was the latrine, which he cleaned out himself.

One day, Pierre said it was time to choose a pig. He explained that every year one pig was slaughtered to provide food. When the time came, Pierre was no braver than with the chickens. He called on the village veterinarian to do it for him. After the veterinarian left, Pierre cut up the carcass, and Sylvie cured the meat in jars of salt water which she kept down in the cellar. No part of the pig went to waste. Even the blood was used to make blood pudding.

When Pierre announced it was time to "service the sow" and said he knew of a farmer who had a hog for that purpose, Régine volunteered to accompany him. She had no idea what was about to happen.

With the help of Sylvie, Pierre tied a rope around the sow's neck. Régine walked it along the road as if it were a dog, while

Marquis ran around barking at their feet. At the farm, Régine had her first lesson in sex.

It wasn't the last. Soon afterwards, Pierre introduced the cow to a bull. That terrified Régine. The bull was enormous and he made a lot of noise. But somehow it didn't work out. The cow seemed as terrified as Régine, so they had to leave and bring the cow back another time.

Régine had been waiting for some time for the sow to give birth. The animal was so pregnant she could hardly walk. But when the birth finally came, it was a surprise. The litter was large, and Régine had to work fast to clear the newborn baby pigs out of the way in case the mother made a mistake and rolled over on top of them. Some of the piglets had trouble getting milk from the mother so Régine learned to feed them from a bottle.

The birth of a calf was more complicated and required the services of the same veterinarian who came to slaughter the pig. Régine was fascinated, but she turned away when he put his hand inside the cow to check the position of the unborn calf.

Régine was particularly fond of sheep even though there were none on the Wathieu farm. Régine had become friends with Irene, the granddaughter of Old Monsieur Bertrand. At seventeen Irene was too old to go to school, so she stayed home to help on her family's farm where there were many sheep. The Bertrands also had a horse, chickens and more cows than the Wathieus. There was even a phone in Irene's house, a luxury that the Wathieu home lacked.

The two girls discovered they had something to share with each other. They both liked knitting. Régine was a good knitter, thanks to Madame André, and Irene knew how to make lace doilies on a circular needle. They got along well despite the gap of six years between them.

At home, Sylvie taught Régine how to spin wool on the spinning wheel in the kitchen, using fleece that she bought from Irene's family. Régine knitted a sweater with this wool, but it was very rough on the skin. Régine also learned from Sylvie how to bake flat country bread and sugar pies. These last *tartes au sucre* were for Pierre because he did not like fruit pies.

The mending was done by a woman from a neighboring village. She came to the Wathieu house to work on a sewing machine which Sylvie kept covered in the main room. Seeing her work reminded Régine of her father and mother sewing "before the war." Another woman came once a month to do the laundry by hand in the sink in the back room. The rest of the housework was done by Sylvie and Régine. Every night as news of German losses came on the radio, it seemed the war would end any moment. But as each day came and there was no word of an end, Régine threw herself into the farmwork. At least for those busy hours, she wasn't lying awake worrying.

Chapter Thirty-six

THE WATHIEU HOUSE had a room that was kept closed. It was meant to be the dining room and a big round table stood in the center, but the Wathieus never ate there. Instead, like Régine's parents, the Wathieus ate in the room that served both as a kitchen and living room.

The newly laid eggs which Régine or Sylvie brought in were put into a bowl on the big table in the closed room. When villagers came to buy eggs, Sylvie went in and counted out the required number. The milk and butter which Sylvie made was kept in the cellar where it was always cool. She would bring up the butter and weigh it on a scale on that same table. At all other times the door to the room was never opened.

It was in this spare room that Sylvie one day divulged a secret to Régine. They had gone in to give it a rare dusting. As they worked, Sylvie told the story in the confiding tone Régine remembered her mother using. Because of that tone, Régine listened in silence.

At the back of the room was a tall cabinet with a glass door. It was filled with plates, glasses, old photographs and other knickknacks. Sylvie opened the glass door and carefully removed all the items one by one, handing them to Régine for dusting. Régine wiped each item with a damp cloth before setting it on the big round table. It took a long time to empty the tall cabinet. Régine examined each piece and was especially interested in the photographs, which were old but well-preserved in heavy frames.

There were photos of Sylvie's nephews and her niece. Her sister, she said, who lived near Liège, had six boys and a girl, and sometimes in summer they all came to the farm for a visit. There were also photos of Pierre's nephew, Victor, who lived in the nearby village of Limont. Victor helped out at harvest-time because he had a horse.

The last item that Sylvie pulled from the cabinet was a jar which had been hidden behind the last of the picture frames, the biggest and fanciest with an elaborate gold trim. The frame carried no picture.

The jar held some sort of liquid and Régine was surprised to see it in the glass cabinet which was reserved for family mementos. It seemed out of place among all the precious items, but Sylvie held it as if it were a treasure. She did not hand the jar to Régine. She held it up to the light and turned it on its side to show Régine what floated in the liquid. Régine leaned forward to take a closer look but could not guess what it was. But she sensed its importance as Sylvie wiped the jar with a damp cloth and placed it gently at the back of the glass cabinet.

"This is the baby I never had," she said.

Régine did not understand.

The mystery only deepened when Sylvie added with great sadness: "It would have been a boy."

In later years, as Régine remembered the pain on Sylvie's face and the sad voice, she understood the significance of the jar and the empty picture frame. Although Régine did not understand at the time, she realized that Sylvie had told her something deeply personal and delicate. Probably even Pierre did not know about the hidden jar. It was something you could only tell another woman. From that day on, Régine felt

130

more like a friend to Sylvie. She also felt more grown up and less of a stranger.

Soon it would be Régine's turn to have a secret revealed.

Chapter Thirty-seven

BY EARLY 1944, the Allies were bombing Europe almost daily. They were doing well in Italy and the Russians were pushing the Germans farther west. But nothing had changed in Belgium. The Germans were still very much in control. Régine's three months on the Wathieu farm were nearing an end but she heard nothing about being moved. Would the man from *Aide paysanne* be coming to get her? Where would they send her now?

Spring was on its way, even though the air was cool. The day began as usual. Régine was awakened by the crow of roosters and hopped off her high bed as the sunshine broke into her room. She looked out the window and saw Pierre head off on his bicycle. Downstairs, Sylvie sat alone at the table. Marquis lay at his usual spot on the floor, and wagged his tail when Régine appeared. "Pierre had to go to to Esneux today," Sylvie said. "He's gone to the *maison communale* to get the ration cards renewed."

The *maison communale* was the equivalent of a town hall for the surrounding area. It was not the first time that Pierre went on an errand in Esneux, but this time Régine had a bad feeling which she could not explain. Was it the mention of the ration cards? That was her only proof that she was Augusta Dubois. All morning Régine could not shake the bad feeling. She was scared.

In the early afternoon, Régine was feeding the chickens

out front when Pierre rode up on his bicycle, his wheels spinning on the few icy patches that still lay here and there on the dirt road. As soon as she saw him she knew something had happened. Sylvie stepped out onto the porch to greet him.

Without looking at Régine or saying a word he went to lean his bicycle against the side of the house. Régine watched, and the bad feeling inside of her grew worse. Pierre turned and stared at her for a minute as if seeing her for the first time. Then he walked away, up to the house.

Régine watched as he spoke quietly to Sylvie. Sylvie looked over at Régine as if puzzled. Pierre called out: "Come over here." Régine noticed he did not call her by name as he usually did. It made the order all the more frightening.

In a daze Régine walked to the porch where the two stood staring at her. Then she heard the question she guessed was coming, the question she feared most, the question she knew she must not answer, no matter what: "Are you Jewish?"

She stood as if frozen, her head bowed, her eyes on the ground. All she could think of were Nicole's words of warning. *Tell no one who you are*. Tell no one you are Jewish.

Then suddenly, it was all too much, too hopeless. She burst into tears.

Pierre continued with another question. "What is your real name?"

Régine covered her face with her hands, turned, and ran crying into the house. She climbed the stairs to her room as if comfort were to be found there, jumped onto her bed and buried her head in the pillow. It was the first time that she had cried so hysterically since she heard about the disappearance of her mother and brother almost two years before, and now it seemed she was crying for them all over again, and for herself.

What was going to happen now? What would Pierre and

133

Sylvie do with her? They could be arrested and shot if the Germans found out they were hiding a Jewish child. They would surely get rid of her as soon as possible. They would contact *Aide paysanne* to have her taken away. She was at the end of her three months, in any case. What had happened at the *maison communale* over the ration cards? What if the Germans already knew and were on their way to the house?

It was too much. She felt so tired. I don't care anymore, she thought.

Her face was so deeply buried in the pillow she did not hear the knock at the door. It was Sylvie.

"Come downstairs. Pierre wants to talk to you." She put her hand gently on Régine's back and repeated, "Come."

Régine dried her eyes and climbed down from the high bed. She walked slowly out of her room, past the basin of holy water, and down the stairs, with Sylvie following.

"Sit down," Pierre said. He sounded worried now — not like when he spoke to her outside. Was it because he was sorry to have to tell her she must go?

"We've reached a decision," he said, sitting down opposite her. "You will stay here with us. We won't tell anyone, except Monsieur Le Vicaire. He will have to know. You will continue to go to church like before, so no one will suspect."

He paused. "We will not have you baptized," he added. "Your parents would not have wanted it."

Sylvie smiled at her and nodded.

Régine closed her eyes and felt a tremendous sense of relief. Then she burst into tears again as Sylvie put her arm around her to comfort her.

"No need to cry," Pierre said. "No need to cry."

Later, Pierre told the story of what had happened at the *maison communale*. He had gone there to renew the ration cards for himself, Sylvie and Régine. The *maison communale* was under control of the Germans, but it was staffed by Belgians.

When the clerk checked the names on the ration cards against an official list that he had in front of him, he found the names of Pierre and Sylvie Wathieu but could not find an Augusta Dubois. After checking again carefully, he looked at Pierre and said in a low, secretive voice: "There is no such person as Augusta Dubois, but here is a replacement card all the same."

Pierre understood immediately. Only Jewish children needed to hide. He gathered up the ration cards and left the office in a hurry. He felt lucky the clerk was a good Belgian like himself who had no intention of turning anyone over to the Germans.

Chapter Thirty-eight

A FEW DAYS AFTER Régine's twelfth birthday in March of 1944, she was awakened early in the morning by Sylvie.

"Get dressed and come down." Sylvie tried to sound gentle but Régine recognized it as an order.

"What is it?" asked Régine, still muddled with sleep.

"There are German soldiers downstairs."

"What!?"

"It's best if you come down and pretend nothing is the matter." Sylvie put her hand on Régine's shoulder to stop her trembling. "It's safer if you do what I say. Just act normal and everything will be all right."

Sylvie left the room, closing the door behind her. Régine climbed out of bed and tried to control her trembling as she got dressed. At the door, she stood for a moment and breathed deeply. Act normal, she told herself. But how do you keep fear from showing? How do you stop shaking?

She took another deep breath and descended the stairs, feeling her body tighten with each step.

Three German soldiers were sitting near the stove. They had their backs to Régine and all she saw were their uniforms which seemed to fill the room. She stared at their big boots, and then at the guns in their holsters.

The soldiers were laughing and talking among themselves in German. Pierre and Sylvie were nowhere in sight. Even Marquis had disappeared from his usual spot on the floor.

Régine waited at the kitchen door and tried to swallow her terror.

The talking and laughing stopped when she appeared. Act normal, she told herself as she stepped forward. The soldiers glanced at her, then turned to each other and went on talking. She decided she should speak.

"Bonjour," she said. Her voice sounded foreign in her ears.

One of the soldiers nodded but did not respond. Sylvie came in from the other room with a bowl full of eggs and set them on the table. Pierre arrived soon after with a milk can which he had filled. Sylvie then went to the cellar and returned with butter which she put on the table. Pierre lit his pipe. It seemed to Régine that everyone was trying too hard to pretend that nothing was wrong. Surely the Germans would notice something strange and start to ask questions. But the Germans went on talking and laughing. Régine should have understood a little because German is similar to Yiddish which she had spoken at home with her mother, but she was too scared to listen, glad they did not seem to pay attention to her.

Then they fell silent and looked around, and Régine felt a stab of new terror. She turned to Sylvie to hide the feeling she had of falling into a deep, black hole.

"Can I help?" she asked in what she hoped was her usual voice.

"No. We're almost finished now," Sylvie said. "These gentlemen are about to leave."

One of them turned to Régine and in German asked her name.

Régine played dumb. *"Je ne comprend pas l'allemand,"* she said, speaking the French words carefully, her eyes lowered.

To her relief, the soldiers turned away and resumed their conversation. Pierre and Sylvie continued to stack the table with food. It seemed to Régine they were taking forever. She wished they would give her something to do. It would be better than standing there, scared and alone with her back to the wall, just staring at the floor.

When were they going to leave?

They seemed to be making themselves more at home. They broke off pieces of bread and began to eat. One held out a piece of bread to Régine. She shook her head and the soldiers laughed. They tried to sound friendly. But Régine felt as if she were back at the Gare du Midi. She saw the soldiers again, pushing Léon into the station. She must not show the fear or anger. She must behave like a country girl who had not seen them take a brother away.

Sylvie brought out bags and filled them with food from the table. Finally the soldiers got up. Two lifted the bags of food and the third carried the milk can. Régine did not look up as they walked out of the room. She listened to the sound of their heavy boots on the floor. Pierre and Sylvie followed them to the front door. Régine heard it open and close, then the sound of their jeep starting up and moving away.

Exhausted, she walked to the kitchen table, fell into a chair, and rested her head on her arms.

Sylvie came up from behind and put a hand on her shoulder.

"They're gone," she said.

Chapter Thirty-nine

T HAT SPRING DAY IN 1944 was the only time Régine saw German soldiers at the farm. From then on, their presence seemed to lessen. With the coming of summer, Hitler's Third Reich was everywhere on the defensive. Her three months at the Wathieus' had long passed. Everyone expected the Allies to land in France any day.

At last, the hoped-for landing took place in June. When this announcement was broadcast, Pierre turned up the volume on the old radio. Pierre and the old men who had come to listen that night, *pour la soirée*, were very excited. The landing at Normandy signaled the beginning of the end of the war.

That same month, the Allies took over the rest of Italy and Russian troops were pushing hard from the east. The Germans were trapped in the giant vise that would ultimately crush them. Every news broadcast brought hope, and Régine, after more than two years of waiting, could actually think about her father returning soon. And her brother. Yes, he would return, too.

But the war was not over yet. The summer of 1944 was a strange and dangerous time. The German army was retreating across Belgium. Some days the fighting seemed closer to Régine than it had been in 1942 when air-raid sirens wailed over Brussels and bomber planes roared above the apartment on rue Van Lint. Other days were so peaceful and uneventful that Régine helped Pierre and Sylvie with chores on the farm without hearing the sounds of distant guns.

The pattern of work was different in summer. A woman still came from another village to do the washing in the back room, but now Régine helped spread the wash on the grass where it was bleached by sunlight. The laundry took a full day and Régine loved the smell of freshly washed clothes.

She helped Sylvie bake pies and fruit tarts using plums and apples from the orchard at the back of the house, and for Pierre they made his favorite sugar pie. Sometimes they baked waffles on a waffle iron.

Régine worked in the fields, spreading dung with a spade and helping to gather beans, gooseberries, raspberries, lettuce and potatoes from the garden. Picking vegetables brought back memories of the early days of hiding when Régine worked in the garden of Madame André and then made jam with her neighbor, Madame Charles.

Every evening Pierre lit his pipe and sat down to read *La Libre Belgique*, which came in the mail. Then the old men knocked on the door and spent the evening by the radio, talking about the war. Régine helped Sylvie peel potatoes for the next day and the cats still gathered for Sylvie to throw them a little piece of raw potato.

Pierre and Sylvie continued to take Régine to church although she resented this more and more. Most of all she resented Monsieur Le Vicaire. Ever since he learned from the Wathieus that she was Jewish it seemed he was on a personal mission to convert her. In church he seemed to address all his sermons to her personally. Sometimes she felt she was the only person there as Monsieur Le Vicaire stared down at her from the altar and described the terrible sufferings that non-believers would have to endure in hell.

That summer, Régine began to menstruate. Sylvie said it

happens to every girl, it makes them women. Régine wondered if her mother had menstruated. She must have, Régine decided, and she felt a sudden longing for her mother that she had tried to keep in control for many months.

The cramps always seemed to start in church during the sermons by Monsieur Le Vicaire. She would hold on, gritting her teeth until the end of the service. Then there was the long trek back to the farm with Pierre and Sylvie. As soon as they were home, she went up to her room, closed the door and lay on the floor until the cramps stopped.

Sometimes the daily routine in Lagrange was broken by the noise of gunfire. Then Régine, Pierre and Sylvie ran into the nearby woods with Marquis limping along close behind. They stayed there until the shooting stopped. A house was a dangerous place. Retreating German soldiers could take it over to hide in and shoot from.

Throughout the late summer of 1944 villagers also came from Lagrange to take shelter in the woods, sometimes staying for hours. Régine met up with her friend Irene and her family among the trees, and the group of them would stand, on the lookout for the rocket bombs that lit up the sky. The new German rocket bombs always took them by surprise. They were called V2s, and approached in deadly silence before exploding with a terrifying noise. At least with the old V1s you could hear them coming.

Brussels was liberated by the Allies in early September. Two months later, all of Belgium was free. American tanks rolled victoriously through the communities of southern Belgium, now liberated from Nazi control. In the tiny hamlet of Lagrange, the advancing troops received a solemn welcome from the farmers and villagers who lined the roadsides, watching with a mixture of anguish and relief.

The soldiers were in a festive mood. Everyone called them "Tommies." They smiled and handed out chocolate and candies to the children who ran up to touch the tanks. Régine, too, got some chocolate, which she had not seen in years. And now she could really hope for the return of her father — and her brother, even.

But the soldiers' celebrations turned out to be premature. When winter came, the Germans launched a counteroffensive in the Ardennes mountains and reoccupied large areas in the southeast of the country, including the province of Liège and the hamlet of Lagrange. This counteroffensive became famous as the Battle of the Bulge. Régine and the Wathieus were again forced to flee into the woods. Since it was winter, they sometimes had to stand for hours in the cold, wrapped in their heavy coats and boots.

The old dog Marquis died. He had worked to the last day of his life, bringing in the cows with Régine. Pierre buried him in the orchard behind the farmhouse and told Régine to go to a nearby farm to pick up a new dog. All the arrangements had been made, he told her. Régine went to get the puppy and carried him inside her coat back to the farm.

"What name shall we give him?" asked Régine.

Pierre scratched his head. "You choose one. I leave it up to you."

Régine thought for a moment. "I know," she said. "Let's call him Tommy."

Chapter Forty

IN JANUARY OF 1945, the last German troops were driven out of Belgium. The liberation brought the long-awaited return of prisoners and survivors of the war. Everyone in Lagrange knew someone who had been reunited with a missing son or grandson. The names of those who returned were broadcast on the radio. Every day, Régine leaned close as the announcer read out the long lists. The lists were broadcast at various times during the day and night. Sometimes she did not move from her chair for hours, even if it meant missing a meal or not milking La Blanque.

"If your father comes back, you will certainly hear about it," Sylvie told her.

But she kept listening, even when the same list was read out a second time, in case she had somehow missed his name the first time.

At the end of April, the radio reported the hanging of Mussolini in Italy. Then the suicide of Hitler as Berlin collapsed before the advancing armies. Finally, at long last, on May 7, 1945, the German commanders surrendered to the Allied leaders. The war in Europe was now officially over. The streets were filled with people celebrating the victory. Soon the returning prisoners and survivors were joined by a stream of soldiers returning from the battlefields. The whole world breathed a sigh of relief that six years of madness and destruction were finally at an end.

And every day, Régine continued to sit by the radio long after the announcer had run out of names. She didn't want to leave the chair even to come to the table for food.

The Wathieus lost patience with her.

"Tell me, what do you hope to accomplish by sitting there?" Pierre asked one night. "You're just making it harder for yourself."

Régine did not respond. How could they say this? Didn't they know her father had promised?

Once Sylvie said the most unspeakable thing of all. Though she asked the question gently, with her hand on Régine's shoulder where she always put it as a gesture of comfort, the words were still terrible: "What if your father doesn't come back?"

Régine exploded. "Of course he will!"

Sylvie was taken aback. "I didn't mean to hurt..." she said, her voice trailing off. But it was too late. The hurt had been done. The question Régine had never asked herself had been asked. As if to ask it was to make it happen.

She had to believe that her father would come back. He would come back and explain everything that had happened. Then she would be with him forever. She had thought of the stories he would tell her of how he had been hiding all this time, how it was too dangerous for him to come looking for her any sooner. Or of how he was captured and had only recently escaped.

There were so many reasons why her father was away longer than anyone. Maybe he had been fighting with the soldiers at the front. Maybe he had been injured and lost his memory for a while. Maybe it was even simpler than that: maybe her father had been searching for her all during the war, but could not find out where she had gone after leaving Madame André.

The stories changed but the ending was the same: her father always came back.

And her brother. Somehow, although she never imagined how as she did with her father, somehow he too would return, even though Monsieur Gaspar's remark about her mother and brother hung in the back of her head like a weight.

"Aren't you happy here with us?" Pierre asked.

Régine did not answer. She just looked at Pierre. Surely he understood. He was not her father. She loved him and Sylvie and was grateful to them both for risking their freedom and maybe their lives to keep her, but only her father's return could make her happy. As time passed, the lists of names of those returning grew shorter and shorter, and Régine became more and more depressed.

Late in May, they were having breakfast one day when someone knocked at the front door.

Pierre turned to Sylvie with a questioning look. It was unusual for a visitor to come to the farm so early in the morning. Régine put down her piece of bread. A strange feeling welled up inside of her, just like a premonition.

The knock came again — loud, confident and somehow familiar.

Pierre got up to answer it. The new puppy, Tommy, followed him. Sylvie got up, too, but Régine stayed at the table and listened.

She heard the front door open.

"Yes?" Pierre said.

"Good morning," said the familiar voice. "My name is Nicole. I've come to fetch Augusta."

Chapter Forty-one

RÉGINE did not want to hear a word of it.

"I'll wait here until my father comes back," she repeated. "I'm not coming back until then."

They were walking up and down the dirt road in front of the house, Régine in her farm clothes and wooden clogs, Nicole in high heels and an elegant skirt and jacket. She had insisted that they go outside to talk so the Wathieus would not overhear what she had to say.

Pierre and Sylvie were as shocked as Régine when Nicole appeared. Perhaps they sensed what was coming. Who was this young woman who carried a briefcase and smoked a cigarette in their presence? They relented a bit when Nicole explained that it was she who had arranged for Régine to live on their farm in the first place, and that she was an old friend of her parents.

Now, away from the house, she explained her plan to take Régine back to the city.

But Régine was not convinced. She, too, was suspicious of Nicole. More than eighteen months had passed since they had parted at the bus station in Brussels. Sometimes Régine had wondered if Nicole had been arrested and deported, too.

It was four months since the last Germans were pushed out of Belgium. Why had it taken her this long to come?

"Why did you never send me a note, a message?" she asked.

Nicole smiled. "There were other children. Hundreds of them. Babies even. I had to find places for them and check they were looked after. And when the war ended, there was the work of getting them back to...to...," she paused, "to relatives. But I knew you were all right."

Régine stopped being angry but it was still a fact that Pierre and Sylvie were the only people who had made her welcome since she left her parents' home three years before.

"I don't want to leave," Régine repeated. "I want to wait here until my father returns."

Nicole did not ask her the forbidden question. Instead she asked her something else: "What have you been learning in school?"

"School?"

"Yes. You have been going to class, haven't you?"

Régine explained how the teacher at the village school had sent her home because there was nothing more she could learn there.

"That is why you should come back to Brussels," Nicole said. "Your father would want you to continue your education. You know that, don't you?"

Régine did not answer. Nicole was right about her father, but how could the Wathieus be left just like that?

Nicole continued: "There's a place waiting for you in Brussels," she said. "It's a hostel for Jewish girls called Les Hirondelles. You'll make friends there."

"Friends?" Régine exclaimed. "That's what you said when I went to the hairdressers'. And you were wrong." Régine looked down at the muddy road. "Pierre and Sylvie are my friends. I love them. And they care about me."

Nicole took hold of Régine's hands and turned the palms upward to show the calluses. "You should be in school, Régine."

"I'm just helping out," Régine insisted, burying her hands in the pockets of her sweater. "They work much harder than I do."

She felt something with her hand in her right pocket. It was small and round and hard like a coin. Then she realized what it was: the blue-enamel medal of the Virgin Mary that Sylvie had given her for protection. Régine's fingers curled around it. It was not something she could show to Nicole, just as she did not dare mention the cross over her bed and the dish of holy water at the top of the stairs and the weekly sermons by Monsieur Le Vicaire. She did not want to give Nicole any more reasons for taking her away.

"No," Régine continued. "I won't go back to Brussels. I'm staying here with Pierre and Sylvie...," she said, then added defiantly, "until my father comes back."

They stopped in front of the house. Régine was sure the argument was over but Nicole did not give up. "Why not at least try Brussels?" Nicole said. "If you don't like it, you can come back here. How does that sound?"

Régine drew a line in the dirt with the toe of her wooden clog. People were always asking her to believe that they knew what was best for her. This time she would be the one to choose.

"You don't have to decide now," Nicole said. "Take some time to think about it. I'll come back in two weeks. Then you'll let me know."

Chapter Forty-two

FOR TWO WEEKS Régine went over Nicole's words. *Why do I keep calling her Nicole? I don't have to anymore. Her name is Fela. Fela Mucha*. She lay awake for hours in the dim light of her room, looking up at the Madonna and child on the opposite wall. The more she thought about it, the more she felt Nicole had a point.

School was not the only reason, but it was an important one. She remembered the conversation she'd overheard years ago in the hallway at the *école primaire*, before Jewish children were banned from public schools. Mademoiselle Descotte had remarked to the other teachers that they would be losing some of their top students. She was one of these. Her father would be pleased to find her in school when he returned. Nicole was right. *Would she ever stop calling her Nicole?*

She also looked forward to meeting other girls. Irene was a good friend, but she was nineteen years old. Régine wanted to meet friends her own age — especially Jewish friends. She missed so many things Jewish: the Yiddish spoken in her home, its stories and songs, her mother's kosher kitchen. All of her father's friends at Solidarité were Jewish — that was the other way to be Jewish, her father's way. It was also Nicole's — Fela's — way. It meant trying to make life better for others. Three years had passed since she was last among her own people. Les Hirondelles would be a good place to start.

But there was another reason to go back to Brussels, and

it was the most important of all. Régine knew from reports on the radio that the Red Cross was working to locate people who had disappeared during the war. If there was any hope of finding her father and brother, of finding out what happened to her mother, surely this international organization could help. She could go to their office in Brussels. She could keep in closer touch, she felt, maybe even meet people who knew something.

After two weeks of thinking this through in the darkness of her room, she made her decision. The next morning she told Pierre and Sylvie.

The couple listened carefully and did not interrupt. They sat, staring at the bread, butter, jam and cottage cheese that were spread on the table. Neither of them touched a bite while Régine spoke. They did not try to change her mind. Instead they showed their usual kindness and understanding.

When she was finished, Pierre said, trying to smile, "If you are not happy there, come back."

"Maybe it won't be forever," Régine added at the end. "If I don't like it, I will come back."

"There will always be a place for you here," Sylvie added.

She promised to write regularly and to let them know immediately if she needed anything.

Régine saw that the Wathieus did not believe she would ever come back.

Régine sat at the kitchen table waiting for Nicole to arrive. Would she ever remember to call her Fela? Would the Wathieus stop calling her Augusta and use her real name? She wore her best dress, and her packed duffel bag lay near the front door. The bag contained all her clothes and her copy of *Uncle Tom's Cabin*. In her pocket was the blue-enamel medal of the Virgin Mary, a memento that would always remind her of Sylvie.

Pierre and Sylvie tried to keep busy as they waited along with Régine. Pierre went in and out of the house on his chores. Sylvie washed and put away dishes and glasses. It was unusual for the Wathieus to look so sad. Even Tommy seemed to be sulking at her feet, as if he, too, felt that she was abandoning him.

Nicole arrived in the early afternoon in a car driven by a friend from Solidarité. She saw immediately that Régine had decided to come to Brussels.

"Ready?" she asked, smiling.

"Ready," said Régine.

Saying good-bye to Pierre and Sylvie was not as painful as Régine had feared. She hugged them and kissed them on both cheeks. Then she turned and walked quickly out the door. She had succeeded in not crying but she did not dare look back. Nicole's friend held open the back door of the car and she climbed in. Nicole joined her in the back seat, and the car made its way along the dirt road past the little village.

For a long time no one said a word. Régine looked out the window at the passing countryside, and felt very alone with her thoughts of the good people she was leaving behind. She told herself that she had made the right decision in leaving Lagrange, but somehow that did not make her feel any better.

Chapter Forty-three

WHEN THEY ARRIVED at Nicole's — Fela's — flat in Brussels, they were greeted at the door by someone else from the past. It was Edgar Herman, whose bicycle she had guarded when he came to visit her father. It was at his flat she had first seen Fela during a Solidarité meeting. As he put his arms around her and smiled in welcome, she already felt closer to her family.

"You will stay here with us for a few days before going to Les Hirondelles," Fela said.

Edgar and Fela seemed determined to cheer her up. The first afternoon, they sat on the terrace of an outdoor café and scooped up large bowls of ice cream. The next day, they took her to an amusement park where they climbed into bumper cars and crashed into each other around the track.

On the third day, Fela started the search for anyone who knew what happened to Régine's family.

They went to the Red Cross by tram. There Régine filled out forms and listed the names of her family: her father, her mother, her brother, Oncle Zigmund and Tante Ida. She wasn't sure about Oncle Shlomo in England. Was he still alive? The Germans had said that London was bombed to the ground. But she added his name, anyway.

"If we hear anything," the official said, taking the sheet from her, "we'll get in touch." He nodded and tried to look sympathetic, but he must have said it so many times before to so many others that his voice sounded mechanical.

On their way out Régine turned desperately to Fela. "Somebody must know something," she cried.

"We'll find out whatever we can," Fela said.

The next few days, Fela became a whirlwind of activity. As they went on the search around Brussels, Régine thought: this is how Fela must have been during the war, when she was Nicole. Picking up children. Convincing parents to give them up. Finding places for them. Taking them there. Checking on them. And all the time, being so kind and understanding. No wonder parents trusted her with their children.

The first stop was 73 rue Van Lint. Régine felt a mixture of pain and excitement as she rode the tram along the cobblestone street with Fela. She gazed out the window as they passed familiar shops and homes. Little had changed on the surface of the neighborhood since she had left the apartment three years before. Soon the old building came into view, and it looked just as she remembered it. Even the café downstairs was open for business.

They got off and stood in front of the building. Régine looked up at the windows of the apartment. The same old curtains were still there, and the place looked lived in.

"Why don't I go in first?" Fela suggested. "You wait here."

Régine nodded. She was afraid to move. She stood looking up at the windows until Fela returned.

"There is no one left who knows anything," she reported. "Even the old neighbors are gone."

Chapter Forty-four

THEN FELA TOOK Régine to Solidarité. The group now met in a small hall, not in the homes of members.

If anyone knew what had happened to her parents, it would be there. They gathered — those who had survived the war in hiding and the few who had returned from the concentration camps — to find comfort in each other.

Régine looked forward to seeing her father's friends from the old days, friends like Edgar Herman. But when she entered, they were all strangers. She tried to connect these faces with any she remembered. The few who had come back* had been released from Auschwitz in January, six months before, when the Russians entered the concentration camp. But they still stood out from the others in the meeting hall. Régine did not need to see the numbers tattooed on their arms to spot them: the large eyes in the hollow faces marked them apart. If her father, *when* her father, came back, would he look like this? Would she recognize him?

She walked slowly through the group. Fela introduced her: "*C'est la fille de Miller.*" That was what they had called her — Miller's daughter — when she had gone with her father to the gatherings before the war. She asked her question: "*Avez-vous vu mon père?*" Have you seen my father?

One by one, they shook their heads. Afterwards, it seemed

---

* Of the 25,475 Jews from Belgium deported to the German concentration camp at Auschwitz in Poland, only 1,335 returned.

to Régine it was as if she had been asking the same person the same question over and over. All had looked at her the same way. All the eyes had shown the same pain. All had shaken their heads without speaking, as if no words existed that would help.

That evening Régine told Fela why she was so sure her father would come back, about Monsieur Gaspar's visit to Madame André. "He said my mother and brother were no more. But he never mentioned my father..."

Fela interrupted her, puzzled. "But he could not have known what happened to them. Nobody knew then."

"But would he have said such a thing if he did not know?" Régine asked. "And in Flemish, which he didn't think I understood?"

Fela was angry. "Well he's dead now, so we can't ask him. How would he have known then what happened to your brother after he was sent to France?"

Régine nodded, excited: "Yes, he could have escaped, couldn't he? He was young and strong. He could have jumped off a train. He could still come back."

Fela lowered her head and said nothing.

"My mother was so sick," Régine went on, "I didn't think she could live through it. That time she went to the hospital, when I saw my father cry, that's when I felt she might not..."

Fela put her hand on Régine's: "Tomorrow, we will see if we can find out more," she said and lit a cigarette.

"Why do you smoke?" Régine asked.

Fela shrugged. "I started after my husband was arrested."

"Oh," Régine said. "I didn't realize..."

"Right on the street, in front of my eyes. Two Gestapo men in black suits came up to him with a gun."

"Did he — did you ever...?" Régine did not know how to put the question.

155

Fela understood. "No," she said. "Taking care of the children helped. So did smoking."

Régine suddenly realized how little she knew about Fela, except that she had come from Poland and been a member of Solidarité like Régine's father. It had never occurred to her that Fela might have been married and that her husband might have been arrested and sent away to a concentration camp. She was glad that Fela had found someone else in Edgar Herman.

"Do you still have relatives in Poland?" she asked.

"Had," Fela said, holding the cigarette tightly to stop the trembling in her hand. "All my family."

"Have you heard from any of them?" Régine was afraid as she asked the question.

Fela shook her head, then shook it again as if to shake off the thoughts. Régine felt a moment of shame that all the time she had been so taken up with her own family it had never occured to her to ask Fela about hers.

But Fela stood up abruptly and put out her cigarette in an ashtray. "Time for bed," she said firmly. "We have a big day ahead tomorrow."

Feeling sorry for herself is not in her nature, Régine decided.

They returned to Solidarité and this time Régine saw someone she recognized: Madame Sadowski, the family friend who had mixed up her mother's separate dishes for dairy and meat so many years before. She and her husband had survived the war, hid by neighbors. Régine was so happy to see them.

But the information Madame Sadowski gave her about her parents was almost worse than not knowing. "The Gestapo raided the building. They took your mother from her bed," Madame Sadowski told her. "The next day they came back and found your father hiding in the coal closet."

Régine listened in disbelief. She was too stunned to answer. It wasn't possible.

Régine cried all that night. What Madame Sadowski had told her could not be true. She could not imagine her father hiding while her mother was taken away. It did not make sense. He had refused so often to leave her mother when she begged him to try to escape to England. What had really happened?

Chapter Forty-five

THE NEXT VISIT was to Jeanne Demers, who had shared the floor above the Millers at 73 rue Van Lint with another family. She had moved out of the building before the Gestapo raid, but her father had gone on living there until his death. Monsieur Gaspar, again. The man who had arranged with her father for her to stay at Madame André's, who had come instead of her father that awful Sunday and spoken the terrible words in Flemish. Régine connected him with bad news and even though he was dead she wondered if more bad news was to come.

But Jeanne Demers greeted her at the door with a reassuring embrace. "I am so glad to see you," she said, excited. "I have something for you."

She brought out a shoebox and handed it to Régine. "I thought that when your family came back after the war, you would want these things."

Régine's hands trembled as she took the box. What was inside?

"As you know," Madame Demers turned to Fela for confirmation, "the Gestapo put seals on the doors after they took people away. But vandals broke into your apartment and took anything of value. My father picked up these few things from the floor and gave them to me to keep for..." She paused as if she was not sure how to end the sentence, then added, "For whoever came back."

158

Régine removed the lid of the box slowly and placed it beside the box. Fela and Madame Demers watched as she lifted out the first items — the mortar and pestle her mother had brought from Poland. As Régine held them in her hands, she could see her mother standing near the stove grinding almonds just before the apartment filled with the smell of baking cookies.

Régine took a deep breath to control the trembling of her hands as she put the mortar and pestle on the table and went back to slowly removing the contents of the box.

What remained were family photographs and each brought a painful memory. There was a small copy of her parents' wedding picture that had hung on the bedroom wall. Régine had looked at it so often when her mother lay ill on the bed beneath it and during the days she spent at home when Jewish children were no longer allowed to go to school. Now as then, she thought how beautiful her parents looked in it.

Then there were snapshots. Was she five or six when she walked hand in hand with her father? She was even younger in another photograph that included her mother and Léon as well. How strong and healthy her mother looked then! And Léon? A photo of him just a year or two before his sixteenth birthday and his terrible disappearance into la Gare du Midi.

Fela and Madame Demers watched in silence, not moving, as if the emotion that Régine was controlling, controlled them. Régine looked at each picture a long moment, in a kind of rhythm of remembrance, before placing it with the others neatly and carefully beside the box.

But one picture suddenly broke the rhythm, for the memory it aroused was too powerful. It was the portrait of herself, smiling at the camera, wearing a flowered dress with the Star of David sewn onto it. She remembered walking with her father to the photo studio of Pierre Dietens. Again she heard her father promise that someday they would go back to have another picture taken, this time with the red side of the star showing.

Remembering her father's promise, she wanted to cry out, to beg him to come back to keep his promise. Instead, she put the picture back into the box, then the others along with the mortar and pestle and replaced the cover. Then she stood up, and in a quiet voice, thanked Madame Demers and moved to the door with Fela following.

When they arrived at Fela's apartment, she calmly emptied the box once more and transferred the contents to the duffel bag she would be bringing to Les Hirondelles.

During the two days left before Régine was due at the hostel Fela continued to help in the search for people who had known her parents. Régine remembered her father had given a non-Jewish acquaintance his radio and sewing machine for safekeeping after the Germans prohibited Jewish people from owning these items. The understanding had been that the man would return them after the war. Fela took her to the man's house but he refused to let her in.

"I don't know you," he said. "Or your father. Nobody gave me anything."

"But I remember," Régine protested.

"Then go to the police," the man said and closed the door on her.

A happier discovery was the Saktregers, the family of Léon's friend who had the same name as her brother and had been his best friend. All four of them had survived the occupation.

Madame Saktreger was happy to see Régine. She kissed and hugged her like a daughter. But she did not talk about how they had escaped the Nazi raids.

"We hid out all over the place," she said, then changed the

subject quickly. "But tell me about yourself."

She does not want to hurt me, Régine realized, and it would hurt me to hear how they all escaped while my family was taken. She particularly envied Maurice because he was her age, and he had his father, his mother and his brother. But she was grateful for the genuine warmth Madame Saktreger showed her, for the invitation to stay for dinner and to come back often, and for the parting embrace and assurance: "You are always welcome in our home." Régine did not mention her parents and Madame Saktreger asked no questions.

Régine did not realize then that she was behaving like most of the Jews in Europe who had survived the war. They did not talk about their experiences and they did not ask questions. Whether they had passed through the horror of the death camps or the terror of being caught while hiding, to talk about it was to relive it or cause others to relive it, and release emotions too intense to be dealt with.

Chapter Forty-six

FELA TOOK RÉGINE to the hostel of Les Hirondelles the next day. The building at 6 boulevard Jules Graindor with its large double front doors was severe and uninviting. Régine was looking forward to being with other girls her own age, but as soon as she entered, she felt uncomfortable.

Fela introduced her and left her "in the good hands of *la directrice*," but *la directrice* seemed more interested in Régine knowing the rules than in making her feel welcome, and she had an odd habit of ending every sentence with "*n'est-ce pas?*" as she gave them out. She also reminded Régine of Madame André in her inability to smile.

"You will sleep here, *n'est-ce pas?*" she said, as they entered an upstairs dormitory. It was crowded with bunkbeds placed so close together, there was barely room to move between them. Régine wondered where she would keep her clothes.

"Here," *la directrice* said, "all possessions are shared, clothing, books, everything." She pointed to a communal dresser: "Socks with socks, sweaters with sweaters, skirts with skirts. You will keep it organized, *n'est-ce pas?*" She motioned to Régine to unpack and left.

As Régine unpacked her duffel bag and put her clothes in the dresser, she felt resentment rising. She had few clothes, but they were hers. Why should she go through a pile each day to find something that fit? When she took out her copy of *Uncle Tom's Cabin* with Fela's note of *Je ne t'oublie pas*, she felt outright revolt. The book and message had meant so much to her during the days when she felt completely alone and she was not about to give it up. She stuffed it back into her duffel bag along with the shoebox of precious photographs and her mother's mortar and pestle, and pushed the bag under her bed.

Downstairs she learned more of the rules from *la directrice*. "You are only thirteen, *n'est-ce pas*? An older girl, *une grande*, will be assigned to look after you. You are allowed out twice a week: on Saturday afternoons and on Sundays if you have friends to visit. You must be back by eight o'clock, *n'est-ce pas*?"

She was relieved later in the afternoon as the girls returned from school or work to find that *la grande* assigned to her was a good-natured girl named Edwige who was not interested in bossing her around.

About fifty girls lived in the hostel. A few of the older ones had come back from the concentration camps, but most, like Régine herself, had passed the war in hiding. Nearly all had been orphaned.

Rosa was an exception. Her father had come back from a death camp and he came to visit her at the hostel. The first time Régine saw him, he looked as haggard and miserable as the survivors she had met at Solidarité. But how lucky Rosa is to have him, Régine thought.

She still hung onto every possibility that her own father and brother would return — even though the concentration camps were empty and it was months since lists of survivors were broadcast. She heard there were still prisoners in Russia. Maybe that's where they were and couldn't let anybody know.

School, the other reason Régine had come back to Brussels, turned out to be a disappointment, too. When asked her favorite activities, she mentioned that she enjoyed creating things with her hands. As a result she was put into an *école professionnelle*, a technical school where the emphasis was on cooking and sewing, not on academic studies. This was not what her father would have wanted for her, she was sure.

Even though she liked the girls and made friends, she noticed from the first day the same silence she had found outside concerning how each had passed the war. Beyond a few words, "She was in a camp" or "I hid out," no experiences were shared and no questions were asked. No one asked Rosa what camp her father had been in and what it had been like. No one asked anyone about their families. The word "parents" was never used.

It was as if each had decided privately she must not talk about the past, as if that was the only way to survive it and not go mad with grief or anger. The girls even seemed to Régine to overdo the act of seeming carefree, laughing and singing too much. They kept it up very well, supporting each other with jokes and stories.

Only during the night did the bravura break down. Memories and terrors kept under control during the day could erupt, frighteningly, as nightmares. One girl woke up so hysterical she had to be taken away by ambulance.

Slowly during the months she was at the hostel, Régine faced the monstrous possibility that no one in her family might return. She had come to Brussels hoping to get news of their survival and to get the kind of education her father would have wanted for her. Neither was working out.

She also resented the silly regulations of *la directrice* who, Régine discovered, was secretly called *Mademoiselle N'est-ce pas* by the girls. She hated the curfews on Saturdays when she was supposed to be back earlier than Edwige when they went out together. Each time she broke curfew she was called into the office of *la directrice*.

On Sundays she visited Fela and Edgar, the Saktregers, or Madame Sadowski, but it was not like living with a family. After a particularly nasty confrontation with *la directrice*, she made a decision and went to inform Fela.

"I want to go back to live with Pierre and Sylvie."

They loved her and she needed that love. When her father or brother came back — she still refused to say "if"— Fela would know where to find her.

Chapter Forty-seven

IN THE LONG WINTER OF 1945-46, everything at the farm was familiar yet different.

The war in Europe had been over for half a year and Régine no longer had to pretend to be someone else. This time she did not travel with a stranger but made her own way by train and bus as far as Limont where the Wathieus came to meet her, like proud parents meeting a returning daughter.

It was two years almost to the day since the first time she had been taken to the little hamlet of Lagrange. It was winter again in Liège and the dirt road that ran from the village to the farm was frozen and covered with icy patches, just as on that day in 1943. When the farm appeared in the distance, Régine felt she was traveling backward in time.

Pierre and Sylvie were exactly the same, too. Pierre wore a jacket over his shirt and trousers. Sylvie wore a dark skirt almost to the ground. On their feet were the same wooden clogs. In the kitchen the three sat down at the table to some freshly baked bread with jam. Bricks were warming in the oven, just as in the old days, and Tommy, the dog, was asleep on the floor. But other things had changed. Régine had become a young woman. Pierre and Sylvie noticed and re-marked on it.

As Régine looked around the familiar room, she saw something new on the wall near the clock and crucifix. It was a gold-framed certificate with fancy lettering. She went over for a closer look and read the names of Pierre and Sylvie Wathieu and the inscription: *pour leur service à la patrie en temps de guerre* — for their service to the country in time of war.

She turned, smiling, to the Wathieus. "Is this because of me?" she asked.

The couple smiled back. "We're not heroes," Pierre said, proud but embarrassed. "We only did what was right."

"We are more honored to have you back in our home," Sylvie added. "This means more to us than any award. You're our daughter now."

Régine did not answer. She did not know how to tell them she would never be a daughter to anyone, except to her own parents.

The subject of adoption was never discussed openly because in the minds of Pierre and Sylvie, there was nothing to discuss. Régine had returned to them. She would become their adoptive daughter. She would be baptized, sent to catechism lessons and confirmed as a Catholic. Then they would legally adopt her.

She lay awake that first night, thinking for hours about religion. How could anyone believe there was a god? If God existed, why did He allow the concentration camps to exist? Why did He permit so much horror? She had made a promise to herself that if her father came back, she would believe in God. But he hadn't come back. No, she decided. She could not believe in God. Not my mother's God, even less the God of Pierre and Sylvie.

How could she say this to the Wathieus? They were good people. They loved her. But they would never understand.

The following Sunday she went to church with them just as she had done when she was Augusta. But after that, she made up excuses not to go. She pleaded menstruation pains when she could.

Other times, on a Saturday night she developed a painful headache. She would go downstairs into the kitchen on a Sunday morning and announce that she was too sick to have breakfast, and then go back upstairs to bed. When she heard the door close downstairs, she jumped out of bed and looked out the window to see Pierre and Sylvie walking alone along the dirt road toward the village church. Did they believe her?

Miraculously, her headaches disappeared by Sunday evening. That was when the village held a weekly dance. The hall was decorated with streamers, a band played accordion music, and all week Régine looked forward to being asked to dance.

She wore her best dress and went with Irene, who was now twenty years old and used to dancing. Pierre and Sylvie took turns serving as chaperons. They sat in chairs along the wall facing the dance floor, and kept watch on the boys who approached Régine. She preferred Pierre as chaperon because he let her stay later at the dances than did Sylvie.

At such times she did not mind Pierre and Sylvie thinking of her as their daughter. She liked being back with them and helping them in the farmwork, although she no longer had as much time for it. Fela had agreed to her going back to live with the Wathieus on condition she continue her education. The closest secondary school was a two-hour bus trip every day and there was homework to do.

If only she could go on living with them without being baptized or adopted, but they kept making references to the adoption. Four months had passed since she had returned to the farm and she did not think she could stall much longer.

On March 16, 1946, she had her fourteenth birthday. A few days later she was looking out the window and she saw Irene ride up on her bicycle. Irene came in out of breath, almost too excited to speak. The Wathieus had no phone and had arranged for Irene's parents to take urgent messages. Irene now had such a message. A woman had called from Brussels trying to reach Régine.

"She wants you to call her back as soon as possible," Irene said. "It's something about your family."

Régine and Sylvie hurried to the house at the end of the village to make the return call. The phone rang twice, then three times. Finally Fela's voice came crackling over the wire. At first Régine did not understand and Fela had to repeat the news: *Oncle Shlomo had been found*.

It was not clear who had found whom, but that hardly mattered. Just as Régine had given the International Red Cross her uncle's name, he had done the same in England in the hope of locating members of his sister's family.

Chapter Forty-eight

RÉGINE SAT AT THE FRONT of the airplane. She was nervous and unable to eat the food brought by the stewardess. She sat upright, unable to relax. It was her second trip over water, but her first time on an airplane.

She reached under the seat and pulled out her duffel bag. She had packed her most prized possessions: the mortar and pestle, her copy of *Uncle Tom's Cabin*, the photographs. She looked through the photographs again. Would she ever know exactly what happened to Léon? To her mother? To her father? Slowly during the last months she had been at the Wathieus' she had come to accept that none of them might return. Information of what went on in the German concentration camps was coming out, horrible and unbelievable, but forcing acknowledgment.

She was looking for something else, and now she found it — a small autograph book.

She put the duffel bag away and opened the book to the first page and read the entry:

> *Never forget*
> *that life is a daily struggle.*
> *Never give in to despair.*
> *Disappointments that we may have*
> *teach us better to deal with life.*
> *Faith in a better world*

is a great force for Man and his endeavors.
Don't take to heart the momentary failures
As long as you are certain of reaching your goal.

Fela
Edgar

Régine smiled, thinking how fat Fela had become, until Fela explained laughing that she and Edgar were going to have a baby.

The three of them had hugged and kissed on the tarmac and promised to keep in touch. Her last sight of them through the porthole had been comforting. They looked so happy together. They will always be my friends, she thought. They bring me closer to my father.

She had sobbed quietly to be leaving them as the plane moved off, taking her to an unknown country.

Pierre and Sylvie had also cried when she left them. Despite their differences, they too would remain friends for life. Régine promised to visit them every time she went back to Belgium. She would never forget all they had done for her.

When Fela's phone call came, they knew immediately what it meant: this time they had really lost their little girl. They also understood it was right that Régine should leave, even though her father had not been found.

"You will be with your family," Pierre said. "That's where you belong."

Although Régine was sad to be leaving Pierre and Sylvie, she was also enormously relieved not to have been baptized a Catholic. Her family had suffered and died because they were Jewish. She must not forsake their memory.

Régine stayed again at Les Hirondelles while she went about collecting all the necessary papers for her departure. The Joint Distribution Committee, an aid organization, gave her money to buy a suitcase for her trip. She was relieved to find that *la directrice* had been replaced by someone else, who did not say "*n'est-ce pas?*" all the time. Rosa was still staying there, too, and she and Régine went to the photography studio together to have a souvenir picture taken of themselves.

When she visited the Saktregers to say good-bye to them as well, she learned that Léon hoped to go to England to study and maybe stay there. Régine hoped so; it would be nice to have someone from her childhood there.

Régine felt much anxiety about going to live in England. When she last saw Oncle Shlomo, she had only been four years old. Whatever she knew about him she had learned from the many stories her mother used to tell. Fela had been reassuring. Régine would be in her own family, she reminded her, and they would send her to school. She could speak Yiddish with them until she mastered English. Yiddish was the language Régine had spoken with her mother, and by now she had almost forgotten it.

Régine looked out of the window of the airplane. Clouds blocked her vision of what lay below. She settled back in her seat, but her back felt rigid, and she was still unable to relax. She flipped the page of her autograph book and read the second inscription.

April 12, 1946

To our daughter Régine,

You are leaving us, dear Régine, taking with you the undying affection of your adoptive parents and leaving behind you enormous regrets. May our best wishes accompany you over there. Be happy and keep with you an everlasting souvenir of us. Do not forget us. We will always remember our dear daughter Régine brightening our home with her beautiful youth.

With the fervent hope that each year will bring you back to us, dear Régine, this comes with our most tender kisses.

Pierre & Sylvie.

Régine noticed something now that she had not seen before, something surprising. It was not so much that Pierre and Sylvie called her their daughter and thought of themselves as her adoptive parents. What surprised her was that they had written "Régine" in her book. This was new, and at first it came as a shock. To Pierre and Sylvie, she had always been Augusta Dubois, right up to their last good-bye. But now, she saw, they accepted that Augusta was gone from their lives and had been replaced by Régine.

The propeller plane hit an air pocket and made a sudden drop. Régine caught her breath, frightened, until the plane evened itself. She looked out the window again. The clouds had opened and she could see the dark water below. They were crossing over the English Channel. She smiled, realizing what day it was: April 15, 1946, the eve of Passover.

Afterword

IN ENGLAND, Régine lived with her uncle, learned English, finished secondary school, took a secretarial course and went to work.

At the age of eighteen, she married Peretz Zylberberg, a survivor of the Buchenwald concentration camp. "I wanted to start a family of my own as soon as possible," she says. A son, Philip, was born in 1952 and a daughter, Sonia, in 1954.

Léon Saktreger who had also immigrated to England remained a close friend. "I saw him and his wife often. He became my surrogate brother." Régine also kept in touch with her friends in Belgium, returning there every holiday. She brought her son Philip to visit the Wathieus and Fela Herman and then, before immigrating to Canada in 1958, she brought both her son and daughter to say good-bye to them.

Through the years, Régine continued to hang onto hope that somehow somewhere her father or brother had survived — even after the Memorial National des Martyrs Juifs erected in Brussels in 1970 listed their names among the 23,880 Jews from Belgium who did not return from the death camps. In 1972 she went to Israel, a present she made herself for her fortieth birthday. She did not believe in God, but she wrote a note and inserted it into the Wailing Wall in Jerusalem, pleading for a miracle. In 1979 another monument was added to the National Memorial in Brussels, this one listed her father among the 242 Jewish heroes who had taken part in acts of resistance to the Nazi occupation and died.

It was not until 1982 that she was forced to abandon all hope. That year German SS files were published with the names of Jews from Belgium who had passed through the Malines deportation center near Brussels, the number of the convoy that took them to Auschwitz and the number assigned each victim. There she found the names and numbers of her father, her brother, her Aunt Ida and Uncle Zigmund — and her mother.

Seeing her mother's name with a number beside it brought a new shock of horror. Because her mother had been so ill, Régine had thought death might have come mercifully to her as soon as she was arrested — before being thrown onto trucks and trains, before her arrival at Auschwitz, before being put into the selection line that sent those unable to work directly to the gas chambers. "I cried more for my mother," she says, "than for any of the others."

Another pain of not-knowing that Régine had carried with her through the years was relieved two years later.

It concerned Madame Sadowski's account of her parents' arrest. Régine had refused to believe that her father could have allowed her mother to be arrested while he hid in the coal closet. But what exactly had occurred when the Gestapo came to 73 rue Van Lint?

In 1984, on a visit back from Canada to England, she was spending an evening with Léon Saktreger and his wife. He was nearly sixty years old at that time. After dinner, Léon handed her a dozen typewritten sheets, explaining: "I felt I should write down what happened to my family and our friends during the war, just so my children and grandchildren might know. I mention your parents in it, so I thought you might like a copy."

Régine tore the papers from his hand and rushed through them to find the part about her parents. She read it, then looked at Léon with astonishment. "Why did you never tell me all this?" she asked. "All these years, you knew this and you never told me?"

"I thought you knew," he answered, flustered. "If you had asked..."

"Tell me now, everything."

Léon started slowly. "After your brother was sent to France, my parents were afraid I'd be picked up next. They made plans for where I would hide. Then came the raids at Antwerp in the middle of August where whole families were taken, and my parents arranged hiding places for themselves as well. Solidarité was telling everyone to try to escape or hide. Your father was telling everyone. But he could not hide himself."

Léon seemed uncertain how to continue. "You did know that your mother had cancer, had been operated on and was sent home from the hospital to die?"

"Yes."

"There was no way she could run and hide and your father was not going to leave her. Your mother was sure she would not be arrested. Why would the Gestapo want a dying woman? She even had a certificate from the surgeon at the hospital stating that under no circumstances should she be moved and she was sure that would save her. It was your father who was in danger.

"My mother was there nearly every day and they told her their plan. If the Gestapo came, your father would hide in the coal closet in the hall and your mother would lock him in with a heavy padlock on the outside of the door. Your mother felt she could walk the short distance to lock him in and let him out afterwards. The Gestapo would not bother to break it open and look inside. Why would anyone be in a closet with a lock outside?

"It was an ingenious scheme," Léon paused. "But your parents underestimated the Gestapo. They took your dying mother from her bed. The next day they came back. We think the new tenant upstairs informed the Gestapo. They found your father, banging on the closet door, trying to get out."

Léon spoke slowly as he completed the account. "At what point your father realized your mother was not coming to let him out, whether he thought she had become too terrorized from the raid to move, whether he knew she had been arrested, we'll never know."

That was all Régine was able to learn about the disappearance of her family in the Holocaust.

In 1991, she attended the First International Gathering of Children Hidden During World War II. More than 1,600 from twenty-eight countries came to New York City for the meetings.

Afterwards, Régine commented: "Many were babies and too young to remember their parents when they were in hiding. I felt sorry for them. I had my memories."

Appendices

Belgium and the Jews

Belgium is justly proud of its record in trying to protect Jews from deportation to the Nazi concentration camps during the occupation of that country by the Germans.

Of the more than 60,000 Jews living there at the outbreak of World War II, more than half survived because of the assistance given by the Belgian people and their institutions in assisting escapes or, more often, in providing hiding places.

Jewish children hid in Belgium

More than 4,000 Jewish children were hidden in institutions and private homes. The sixty-five schools, convents, orphanages, creches, camps and hospitals that provided this shelter knew the origin of the children they were taking in and the danger of being found out by the Gestapo. Hundreds of private families also gave shelter to one or two Jewish children, some knowingly, most unknowingly. Jewish children were mixed in with non-Jewish children by Belgian organizations providing "country stays" for city children.

Solidarité Juive

Solidarité was one of several communist organizations in Belgium at the time of the outbreak of World War II. The Communist Party was outlawed and non-citizens were forbidden to participate in political activity of any nature but many Jews from eastern Europe were communists and believed that communism would end the racial and religious prejudice that seemed endemic in that part of the world. Because organizations like Solidarité and Secours Mutuel, a leftist Zionist organisation, operated on a personal level in small groups in private homes, publishing and distributing underground newspapers, they were immediately effective in proposing opposition to the Nazis, advising Jews not to register, not to answer call-ups, warning them of impending raids, and recommending they go into hiding.

As the arrests and deportation of Jews mounted, the Comité de Défense des Juifs was formed in 1943, uniting a wide spectrum of Jewish political and cultural groups. They were assisted by an equally wide range of non-Jewish Belgian organisations, leftist, humanitarian and Christian.

Fela Mucha-Herman, alias Nicole alias Marie-Solidarité

Fela Mucha was a *convoyeuse*, one who picked up the Jewish children from their parents, took them to hiding places, checked that they were properly looked after, and following the war, returned them to parents or other relatives who survived or found sanctuaries for them. As soon as the first arrests of Jews took place, all her waking hours were devoted

179

to saving children. Still a believing communist at war's end, she and her second husband, Edgar Herman, and their son and daughter moved to Poland to help build the great new socialist state. "By our second day there, I was completely disillusioned," she remarked shortly before her 80th birthday in 1994. "Anti-semitism, corruption, greed, bribery, favoritism were even more rampant than when I left Poland in 1938." It was six years before she and her family could return to Belgium. "Still, I'm glad I was a communist back then early in the war. It permitted me to do the most important work of my life." Several hundred Jewish children owe their survival to her help.

The German Deportations

The names and birthdates of the members of Régine Miller's family, the German convoy that took them from Belgium to Poland, and the number ascribed to each are all taken from German lists published in 1982. All Jews arrested in Belgium passed through the SS army depot at Malines (Mechelen) near Brussels where they were given numbers before being transported to the Nazi concentration camp at Auschwitz.

From the number of the transport, we know that Régine's mother was the first in the family to be picked up by the Gestapo. She was on convoy No.11 that left Belgium with 1,742 Jews, including 523 children, on September 26,1942 and arrived at Auschwitz on September 28. Of these 344 were assigned to work duty and only 30 survived the war. All the others died in the gas chambers.

Her father was on the next convoy (No.12) that left Belgium October 10 along with convoy No.13 carrying 1,679 Jews, of which 487 were children. Only 54 survived.

Her brother Léon, who had been conscripted by the Germans in July and sent as forced labor to build fortifications on the northern coast of France, was returned along with the other young Jewish conscripts to Malines where they were registered and put on convoys No.16 and No.17. They left with 1,937 prisoners, including 137 children, on October 31. At the Belgian-German frontier 241 managed to escape from the train. (Régine liked to believe that her brother had been among them; when he did not return, she thought he might have been shot trying to escape.) Only 85 survived from these two convoys.

Régine's aunt Ida and uncle Zigmund were both on the same convoy—No. 18—that left Malines along with convoy No.19 on January 15, 1943 with 1,632 prisoners, of which 287 were children. Seventy-seven managed to escape at the border. Of the 1,555 who arrived at Auschwitz on January 18, 468 were assigned to work duty. The balance were sent to the gas chambers.

In all 26 convoys left Malines between August 4, 1942 and July 31, 1944, carrying 25,257 Jews from Belgium to the death camp of Auschwitz. An additional two convoys took 218 to other German concentration camps,132 of them to Buchenwald.

World War II in Belgium

On the eve of the Nazi invasion, the Jewish population of Belgium was 66,000 (out of a total population of 8.3 million). Only ten percent of Jews however were Belgian citizens. Most of the others had come from Eastern Europe (mainly Poland) and Germany, escaping the Nazi threat. Thirty-three thousand Jews lived in Brussels, primarily in the district of Anderlecht, near the train station.

There were very close ties between Jewish groups and Belgian leftist movements, and this would prove to be very important in rescue efforts and the (relative) success of the Resistance efforts during the war. A total of 70,000 people were in the Resistance in Belgium. The Comité de Défense des Juifs helped find hiding places for Jews. Their children's branch, Oeuvre Nationale de l'Enfance, hid 4,000 children.

May 22, 1939	Germany and Italy sign pact proclaiming military alliance.
Sept.1-2	Germans invade and occupy Poland.
Sept. 3	Britain and France declare war on Germany.
Oct. 27	Belgians declare neutrality in war.
Jan. 10, 1940	Germans draw up plans to invade Belgium/Netherlands.
Jan. 15	Belgians refuse to allow British/French troops to cross through Belgian territory.
April	Germans invade and occupy Denmark and Norway.
May 10	Germans invade Belgium, Netherlands and northwestern France.
May 17	Germans complete invasion of Belgium; occupation begins.
May 28	Belgian king (Leopold) surrenders.
May	Many Belgian Jews leave (or try to) for France and/or England.
June	Fall of France.
June 10	Italy declares war on France and Britain.
July 17	Battle of Britain begins.
Sept. 17	Beginning of London Blitz.
Oct. 23	"Ritual slaughter of animals" is outlawed by Nazi authorities in Belgium. Arrest of many Jewish "leftists."
Oct. 28	Germans define who is a Jew and enforce Jewish census. Jews banned from public administration, legal, teaching and media positions.
1941	During 1941, more than 40,000 German and Belgian Jews are deported to the Warsaw Ghetto.
May 31	Belgian-Jewish enterprises forced to identify themselves as such; withdrawals by Jews from their bank accounts restricted.
June	Operation Barbarossa, Germans invade Russia.
Aug. 29	Freedom of movement for Jews limited to four major cities (Brussels, Antwerp, Liege, Charleroi); nightly curfew from 8:00 pm to 7:00 am.
Dec. 1	Jews expelled from public schools (implemented four months later

Dec	Japanese attack Pearl Harbor. Americans enter the war.
Jan. 1942	Nightly raids by Allies on France, Belgium, Holland begin.
Jan. 17	Jews are forbidden to leave Belgium.
Jan 20	"Final Solution" drafted at Wannsee Conference, Berlin.
March-April	Liquidation of Jewish businesses.
March 11	Forced labor for Jews decreed; deportations begin many are sent to northern France to construct fortifications along the coast.
April 1	Implementation of public school expulsion.
May 27	Nazis order the wearing of yellow badge in shape of Star of David publicly identify Jews.
June 1	Restrictions placed on Jews practising medicine.
July 22	First arrests of Jews at train station in Antwerp.
Aug. 4	Deportations to concentration camps begin. At first, only Jews who are not Belgian citizens are deported.
Sept 15	Jewish Defence Committee formed. Allies itself with Jewish Communists and Zionist groups. Efforts made to find hiding places, especially for children.
Jan. 1943	Red Army takes Stalingrad and Leningrad, German retreat begins.
Jan. 20	Jean de Selys Longchamps, a Belgian pilot in the R.A.F., bombs the Gestapo headquarters in Brussels, providing a moral boost to all Belgians.
April 19	Start of Warsaw Ghetto uprising.
July 9	Invasion of Sicily by Allies.
March 1944	"Pre-invasion" bombing of northern France, Belgium, Holland: aircraft factories, V-weapon sites.
June 4	British and American troops enter Rome.
June 6	D Day landings in Normandy.
Sept. 3	Brussels and Antwerp liberated by Allies. British and Canadian troo[...] through northern Belgium; American troops through south.
Sept. 8	Italy surrenders to Allies.
Oct.	Allied drive to capture port of Antwerp succeeds; Allies go on to Holland.
Nov.	German V1 and V2 counterattacks in Belgium, Holland. Belgium is liberated by the end of the month.
Dec. - Jan.	German counterattack (Ardennes) in the southeast of Belgium: known as the Battle of the Bulge. Americans attack from west and south, British from north. Fierce fighting accompanied by heavy air bombardments.
Jan. 1945	Liberation of Auschwitz by Russian troops.
Jan. 28	End of Battle of the Bulge. Last German troops leave Belgian soil.
April 25	Russian, American troops meet at Torgau (Germany) to split German armies.
April 28	Mussolini killed.
April 30	Hitler commits suicide.
May 7	Germany surrenders.

Bibliography

Gilbert, Martin, *Atlas of the Holocaust*, London: Michael Joseph Limited, 1982.

Gutman, Israel, ed. in chief, *Encyclopedia of the Holocaust*, Vol I,III, New York: Macmillan Publishing Company, 1990.

Klarsfeld, Serge, *Mémorial de la déportation des Juifs de Belgique présenté par Serge Klarsfeld et Maxime Steinberg*, édité par l'Union des déportés juifs en Belgique et Filles et fils de la déportation, Bruxelles, New York: The Beate Klarsfeld Foundation, 1982.

Pitt, Barrie and Frances, *The Chronological Atlas of World War II*, Toronto: Lester & Orpen Dennys Limited, 1989.

Steinberg, Maxime, *Le Dossier Bruxelles-Auschwitz: La police SS et l'extermination des Juifs de Belgique*, édité par le Comité belge de soutien à la partie civile dans le procès des officiers SS Ehlers, Asche, Canaris, responsables de la déportation des Juifs de Belgique, avenue de la Toison d'Or, 16 bte 3 1060, Bruxelles, 1980.

Steinberg, Maxime, *L'Étoile et le Fusil, Tome I, La question juive 1940-1942*, Bruxelles: Éditions Vie ouvrière, 1984.

Steinberg, Maxime, *L'Étoile et le Fusil, Tome II, 1942 Les cent jours de la déportation des Juifs de Belgique*, Bruxelles: Éditions Vie ouvrière, 1986.

Steinberg, Maxime, *L'Étoile et le Fusil, Tome III, La traque des Juifs 1942-1944*, Bruxelles: Éditions Vie ouvrière, 1986.

Steinberg, Maxime, *Extermination, sauvetage et résistance des Juifs de Belgique*, Comité d'hommage des Juifs de Belgique à leurs héros et sauveurs, Bulletin périodique de documentation No. 4, avril 1979.

Teitelbaum-Hirch, Viviane, *Enfants cachés: Les Larmes sous le masque*, Bruxelles, Editions Labor, 1994

THE DIARY OF A YOUNG GIRL
Anne Frank
Edited by Otto H. Frank and Mirjam Pressler
Adapted for younger readers from the Definitive Edition

The Diary of a Young Girl remains the single most poignant true-life story to emerge from the Second World War.

In July 1942 Anne Frank and her family, fleeing the horrors of Nazi occupation, hid in the back of an Amsterdam warehouse. Anne was thirteen when the family went into the Secret Annexe and, over the next two years, she vividly describes in her diary the frustrations of living in such confined quarters, the constant threat of discovery, hunger and tiredness, and, above all, the boredom. Her diary ends abruptly when, in August 1944, she and her family were finally discovered by the Nazis.

This edition, specially adapted for younger readers from the Definitive Edition, provides a deeply moving and unforgettable portrait of Anne Frank – an ordinary and an extraordinary teenage girl.

READ MORE IN PUFFIN

For children of all ages, Puffin represents quality and variety – the very best in publishing today around the world.

For complete information about books available from Puffin – and Penguin – and how to order them, contact us at the appropriate address below. Please note that for copyright reasons the selection of books varies from country to country.

On the worldwide web: www.puffin.co.uk

In the United Kingdom: Please write to *Dept. EP, Penguin Books Ltd, Bath Road, Harmondsworth, West Drayton, Middlesex UB7 ODA*

In the United States: Please write to *Consumer Sales, Penguin USA, P.O. Box 999, Dept. 17109, Bergenfield, New Jersey 07621-0120*. VISA and MasterCard holders call 1-800-253-6476 to order Penguin titles

In Canada: Please write to *Penguin Books Canada Ltd, 10 Alcorn Avenue, Suite 300, Toronto, Ontario M4V 3B2*

In Australia: Please write to *Penguin Books Australia Ltd, P.O. Box 257, Ringwood, Victoria 3134*

In New Zealand: Please write to *Penguin Books (NZ) Ltd, Private Bag 102902, North Shore Mail Centre, Auckland 10*

In India: Please write to *Penguin Books India Pvt Ltd, 706 Eros Apartments, 56 Nehru Place, New Delhi 110 019*

In the Netherlands: Please write to *Penguin Books Netherlands bv, Postbus 3507, NL-1001 AH Amsterdam*

In Germany: Please write to *Penguin Books Deutschland GmbH, Metzlerstrasse 26, 60594 Frankfurt am Main*

In Spain: Please write to *Penguin Books S. A., Bravo Murillo 19, 1° B, 28015 Madrid*

In Italy: Please write to *Penguin Italia s.r.l., Via Felice Casati 20, I-20124 Milano*

In France: Please write to *Penguin France S. A., 17 rue Lejeune, F-31000 Toulouse*

In Japan: Please write to *Penguin Books Japan, Ishikiribashi Building, 2–5–4, Suido, Bunkyo-ku, Tokyo 112*

In South Africa: Please write to *Longman Penguin Southern Africa (Pty) Ltd, Private Bag X08, Bertsham 2013*